Where does a clown go?

Andrew Rose

ISBN: 978-1-952337-84-0

Cover photography courtesy of *The Los Angeles Daily News*

I would love to hear from you, letting me know what you think of this book: roseinsf@aol.com

For Mom, who loved the circus.

1. DREAM

Dare to dream. Friends, if there's one message this book has to offer, that's it. I dreamed of being in the circus. At seventeen, I had a one-shot proposition, where determination and luck converged. Not all my dreams have come true since, but I live with the comfort of knowing what *could* happen if I put myself out there. I beg you to do the same.

I've established myself *on the outside,* what we used to call a more conventional life, while we were on the road. Education and the pursuit of employment in more traditional forms followed my two years as a clown in the Ringling Brothers and Barnum & Bailey Circus. However, there have also been instances in my twenties and thirties when I followed the siren's call of the sawdust. Over time I've come to accept the fact that the circus, for better or worse, will always be a part of me. This is still the case, even though the Ringling Brothers and Barnum & Bailey Circus ceases to exist as this book is being printed.

The world of the circus, by definition, is one of change. It's anyone's guess whether those who complain are whiny reactionaries or virtuous purists. This was also an issue long ago in the 1956 movie *Trapeze*. A broken-down flying trapeze artist, played by Burt Lancaster, moans in his beer that the *real* circus is gone forever. Interestingly, Lancaster was an acrobat himself in the Kay Brothers Circus, until an injury in 1939 ended his career. He subsequently became a movie star, but it didn't happen immediately. Lancaster made a living as a salesman at Marshall Fields in New York City before his transition to acting. Many years later, in 1985, now an elder statesman in show business, Lancaster hosted *Circus of the Stars*. Between acts he would muse, "Oh, to be young and in the circus. Oh, to be *young*..." Television celebrities presented trapeze, juggling, and animal training on this annual TV special on CBS from 1977 to 1994.

Watching *Circus of the Stars* inspired me, but I can't pinpoint an exact moment when I first became enthralled with the circus. One of my earliest memories is of my sister Lynne reading *Toby Tyler* to me on the couch. This adventurous boy ran away from his foster home to become part of the circus world. Snippets of the book and random scenes from the Disney TV movie still come to surface. A painting in black and gray depicts Toby holding Mr. Stubbs, the chimpanzee he adopted. A skinny, bald-headed conniving boss cheats Toby. A burly elephant handler befriends and protects the boy.

Hazy memories of my first glimpses into this weird, wonderful entertainment form also pop into my mind. I recall sitting in the audience as a toddler, watching elephants tramp on Modesto, California's, minor league baseball field. The elephants were *tailing up*, wrapping their trunks around the tails of those in front of them. I loved watching the baby at the end. One of my favorite books as a small child was *If I Ran the Circus,* by Dr. Seuss. I recall his whimsical drawings and words, depicting almost unfathomable oddities. I even practiced my own *act* for a while in the backyard, diving from a walnut tree onto a pillow I took from my bedroom. I'm fortunate to have not broken anything while doing this.

One summer morning, Mom announced to my sister and me that we were going to Circus Vargas. I asked what it was, and she said she didn't know anything about it, so we piled into the car and made our way up Highway 99 to Stockton's Weberstown Mall. At that time, Modesto, California, was too small of a market for such an attraction. We knew that the half-hour drive would mean something special that we couldn't find in our hometown. Stockton was our frequent family diversion from routine, where we'd enjoy Macy's, Orange Julius, and The Sampan, an all-you-can-eat Chinese buffet. There was even a disc jockey that we could watch through the window downtown at radio station KJOY. I worked there later in my life, selling commercial time.

This time in Stockton was my first visit to the circus, or my first fully conscious visit to the circus. There was a sizable crowd in the lot at Weberstown. This would be one of the summer highlights for California's central valley. We waited in line, and I saw that the portable marquees were announcing THE WORLD'S LARGEST TRAVELING BIG TOP. During the performance I was particularly taken with the unassuming man in a green leotard, starting his swing, getting ready to grab his partners out of the air on the flying trapeze. Mom said something like, "Look at the catcher, all alone up there."

Mom, an exercise fanatic, also thought out loud that she could possibly make her legs look like those of the late middle-aged foot juggler. The ringmaster had announced that the woman had appeared in the movie, *The Greatest Show on Earth,* which had come out some twenty years prior.

I discovered in years to come that Circus Vargas was in many cases a performance venue for those beginning and ending their careers. The show was big enough that I noticed a separation between me and the performers. I think that was when the seed was planted. Somehow, I could become one of *them.* I was told that the kids who performed in the show knew nothing else. Likewise, I recognized that I'd have to leave everything *I* knew to become a part of this world.

I made up my mind that I would have this way of life. At fourteen I typed a letter to Circus Vargas. I inquired about the possibility of helping publicize the circus when it came to Modesto. By now the market of my hometown was considered worthy to support this show. I knew that the circus was on its way and yearned to be a part of it by any means possible. After dinner at Carmen's, a favorite Mexican eatery, Mom, Dad, and I strolled to the car. We passed a vacant retail space, and I spotted through the window in the darkened room, a huge blue poster with *CIRCUS VARGAS* emblazoned in bold yellow caps. I knew it was the advance office.

Surprisingly, someone called me. I was to show up with my juggling equipment at 10 A.M. on a Saturday. This time there was somebody in the office, a thin, unsmiling man with a mustache named Jim. He got right to the point, showing me a black and white glossy photo of a man in greasepaint and costume named Mike, the show's advance clown. Mike seemed perfectly suited for his job. He was burly and middle-aged, with a masculine, friendly voice. A temporary podium was set up in the parking lot to publicize the show, made of white, painted wood. Green Astro-Turf served as the floor. The pseudo stage would accommodate four to five people sitting. Two locals I didn't know were hired to sell tickets. Jim the advance man was there to supervise, while Mike was on hand to stir up excitement. My brief internship would be as Mike's juggling sidekick. We bantered about, and intermittently I'd do a little juggling on the podium. Mike and I walked into Joseph Magnin, a dress shop where my mom was a regular customer, to put on an impromptu show. A lady from behind the counter acknowledged me as *Jerie Rose's boy,* which felt good.

This happened to be the weekend of the Modesto Renaissance Fair. I would put on my tights and do some juggling there. Jim exploited me further, but I didn't care. He sent me to the fair with three stapled Circus Vargas posters, which would stand upright. I can't really say that I was *in* show business; I wasn't paid for my efforts. Still, I figured it was a start.

Mike had confided in me that he had a son himself. He explained that the boy hated the circus because it took his father away from him. Wisely, I didn't pry. Mike said he was going to take me out on the road with him when summer rolled around. It didn't happen. When Circus Vargas came back through Modesto the following year, I asked a clown if he was still with the show. He replied that Mike had left to pursue an acting career. My brief encounter behind the scenes at Circus Vargas made me want this life even more. But first I had to deal with three more years of high school.

I wanted adventure outside of Modesto. The thought of travel appealed to me as much as performing. I had the overwhelming desire to experience life outside of my hometown as soon as I had completed my academic burden. Amish teenage boys experience a period of *Rumspringa*, where they are allowed to experiment with the secular world before committing to the fold. Currently, a *gap year* is in vogue, where young adults will take time after high school before beginning higher education. I had a quest of my own. I can question myself forever on whether I was old enough to embark on a life that was completely foreign to me. Good decision or bad; it's how I started my adulthood.

My last performance as a clown in the Ringling Brothers and Barnum & Bailey Circus came at the end of November, 1985. Many years have passed. Still, there are people who find out about my time on the road and can't wait to hear about it. No matter what I do in life, the circus will follow me. I flash to an image of a gigantic ball that follows a man, known only as Number Six (Patrick McGoohan) in the sixties television show, *The Prisoner.* In my case, there's no reason to feel imprisoned by my own gigantic ball, the circus. It's as much a part of me as my limbs and organs. It may rest dormant for months on end, but the big top spirit recurs when I watch a show, or somebody asks me to recall the good old days.

I did reasonably well in school and participated in an adequate number of extracurricular activities. I felt like an ordinary kid with ordinary capabilities. As the youngest of three children, it seemed that everything I could get involved in had been done before by my brother and sister. That is, except the circus. It was a way to show that I was different. I could have paid more attention in school but dreamed of something else. As freshmen in algebra class, my friend Paul and I schemed about developing an acrobatics act. During our sophomore year we went to see Circus Vargas together, wondering what our future would hold outside of Modesto. After high school, Paul eventually landed a job playing piano in Tokyo Disneyland and then went on to become a lawyer for the Disney corporation.

When I got closer to graduation, I didn't feel any pressure as the Vargas show and other circuses came through town and I tried to latch on. I figured I had nothing to lose and might as well take a stab at it. My mom reasoned there would be no harm in letting me dream. She preferred that I had more dedication to school but was glad that I had passion about something. The pursuit of employment gave me an excuse to come to the midway and soak up the atmosphere. It was a joy to see the big top in my hometown and all that came with it. A friend of mine had printed up some business cards that billed me as a juggler. I started passing them out as an excuse to get behind the scenes. The Big John Strong Circus arrived in Modesto and left without me. So did Circus Vargas. I made the half hour drive to see the Emmett Kelly Circus, a small show that was playing onstage at San Joaquin Delta College in Stockton.

Between performances I asked to see the proprietor, Emmett Kelly, Jr. I tried to avoid being star struck. He had inherited his father's clown face and *Weary Willie* character. Mr. Kelly was kind enough to sit and talk with me backstage, but said, "I'm sorry, son," when I asked him for a job.

As anybody involved in the entertainment industry will attest, rejection is part of the package. I remember Mom bringing up the possibility that she and Dad didn't raise their children with enough toughness for them to be in show business. On the road, I would find out that she had a point. But I still had the lingering hope as my senior year wore on in its dull fashion. When I was a kid, I was impressed with a relatively unknown Illinois congressman named John Anderson running for president as an independent. I had no idea what his platform was. However, I admired how he threw his hat in the ring, with virtually no chance of winning. His slogan was *The Possible Dream.*

My ancestors found a way to make their own dreams possible. On mom's side, Grandpa worked around the clock, tending his local businesses. This included minding orchards and cattle more efficiently than any hired hand was inclined to do. On weekends and summer vacation, he often took us with him. Grandpa loved the work, showing us off to his business associates. Along with his apricots, we were the fruits of his labor. His wife, whom we referred to as *Granny,* loved to hear about my circus travels. She said wanderlust was in my Scandinavian blood.

The great grandparents on my father's side escaped the Czar of Russia. Jewish families, by millennia of training, are conditioned to move on, not dwell on the past. Hence, little information was passed down from my lineage before their arrival on Ellis Island, including my original last name.

My great grandmother, Sophie Berman, arrived in America as a teenager. Her daughter Ida married my paternal grandfather, Irving Rose. Grandma Sophie was the only member of my family who wasn't thrilled with my circus adventure. I suppose in her paradigm I wasn't honoring the risk and sacrifice she made to get here. She was bedridden at the Jewish Home for the Aged in Tarzana, California, when I came to visit her, clearly displeased that I had pursued such a strange career. I like to think she watches over me now and smiles, understanding that I had to make my own odyssey. I am grateful for my strong, stable family roots, which were passed down to my own generation.

Blessed with doting parents, I felt truly invincible. Yet a wave of sadness came over me when I reached first grade. Maybe I wasn't ready. Kindergarten was no problem because it was only a half-day in the afternoon. I'd keep my happy routine, waking up when I wished, exercising with Mom while watching *The Jack la Lanne Show.* My happy life at home, waiting for Mom to finish reading *Hints from Heloise* from the paper, while my can of frozen Welch's grape juice thawed, was uninterrupted. I'd cheerfully skip out the door and check in for the afternoon. Nothing much bothered me, including the older children screaming through the fence, "Kindergarten babies, born in the gravies!" At four, I reminded myself that there was no need to be annoyed by insults that weren't even grammatically correct.

I entered first grade the following fall. The same quarter mile from my cozy house on Leslie Lane became the Bataan Death March. It was all Mom and Dad could do to get me out the door, as I anticipated the horrors of another day sitting at my desk. My sadness bubbled over when I arrived at the school grounds, and I was labeled a *crybaby*. Was life supposed to be like this? Mom chose to be a housewife, but she would have had a brilliant career as a therapist. One afternoon there was a break in the gloom. On the way home from school, I found a little round rock. It was painted yellow, kicked loose from the crosswalk. It was the same crosswalk where I had previously cried because too many cars were keeping me from making my way. A sympathetic state worker in an orange vest advised me to simply wait with patience, and it worked. Another time, I was frightened by a car horn, realizing that I was standing in the middle of the street and hadn't looked both ways. I came home and buried myself in the blankets of the bunk bed I shared with my brother.

This time, with my new bauble, I was miraculously elated. I couldn't wait to show Mom my treasure. She took a ballpoint pen and drew a happy face on it, the kind that was seen in the seventies on metal buttons and t-shirts everywhere. The simple marketing tool reminded Americans to remain happy despite the Vietnam War. It reminded me to remain happy despite the Carroll Fowler Elementary School War. I picked my chin up by any means necessary, which often meant goofing off. Dejection, self-medicated by riling up my fellow students, became a way of life. It seemed I was destined to repeat first grade.

Drew Buie, a relatively unknown football player for the Oakland Raiders in the early seventies, inadvertently played a role in saving my academic career. Dad delighted in announcing to me that *Drew*, in addition to the already-used *Andy*, could be a derivation of my given name, Andrew. By happenstance, our family moved in the middle of my first-grade year from Ceres to Modesto. At six, I used this fourteen-mile change of scenery to straighten up and fly right. Muhammad Ali and Kareem Abdul-Jabaar, both in the prime of their careers, had decided to take on new identities. Why not me? At my new school, I decided to be known as *Drew* and blazed a path of academic excellence. Tall, red-headed Miss Cox, my magnificent teacher, facilitated a newfound desire to learn. Alas, I went back to being called *Andy* in high school, where I promptly began goofing off again. Some lessons need to be relearned.

It's probably futile to pick through my ordinary childhood for precursors to an early adulthood of greasepaint, performance, and travel. I suppose if I developed into a stellar athlete, I'd reflect on days of running and swimming with reckless abandon. If I became a renowned psychologist, I'd possibly recognize as an omen my drawing of Santa Claus burning in a fireplace after coming down the chimney.

But I *did* love, for as long as I can remember, to perform. Recreating vocally the theme of *The Dick Van Dyke Show,* skipping around a chair at the appropriate percussion chord. One of my earliest memories is standing on a wooden stepladder in the kitchen, pretending to be Jim Nabors, singing the opening theme for his show.

An entrepreneurial idea of Dad's inspired me to apply greasepaint and get money for it. I was twelve, and he suggested I dress up as a clown and sell sodas from a wheelbarrow at Modesto's Fourth of July parade. My big sister kindly applied my make-up in front of the bathroom mirror. I sold out at a tidy profit that day and went back to my summer vacation. However, the seeds of professional clowndom were planted.

My consistent need to perform didn't always have favorable results. During my sixth birthday party I climbed a tree in my backyard and yelled, "Look at me!" I raised my arms and promptly fell to the ground. Dad took me to the doctor, while Mom stayed at home to salvage the festivities. I told my father that I couldn't wait to get back home to my party. Dad honestly replied that it would be over by the time we finished our medical errand. Fortunately, my only injuries were being bruised and sad. Mom, years later, related to me there was always something inside that said *look at me*. This character trait, according to her, contributed to my becoming a clown.

Whatever calamities I faced, Mom or Dad would always hear my prayers, tuck me in, and kiss me goodnight. The world was my oyster. I would become anything and everything: pro football player, movie star, champion swimmer, singer, Olympic runner, truck driver, astronaut, circus clown.

I grew older and sadly began to realize my limitations. It seemed I always had to work harder than others. And even then, success would be limited. Joy in running faded upon realizing my pigeon-toed legs wouldn't carry me as fast as my competitors. The simple pleasure of reading waned, as I told myself that my peers were able to absorb knowledge more quickly. Worst of all, I'd cry at night for fear that I'd never comprehend basic math.

A thick-boned *man's man*, George Bratton was my sixth-grade teacher. His claim to fame was having been drafted out of college as a halfback for the Los Angeles Rams. Mr. Bratton would make admonishments that he'd one day open the paper and read about one of us being incarcerated. Wisely, I never applied this technique a generation later; It's a different era for teachers. I also remember Mr. Bratton stating, "No matter how good you are at something, there will always be someone who is better." I thus embarked on the school of hard knocks.

By the time my senior year of high school approached, I was ready for a change. Little and slow, I faced the sad reality that I had no aptitude for the gridiron. Dad made it to the semi-professional level as a football player, and there was nothing more I wanted as a preteen than to follow in his footsteps. A dozen others with more desire than talent also watched from the sidelines, decked out in gear that was seldom used. As each of the two successive years followed, fewer of my bench colleagues were to be seen, avoiding further humiliation. A precursor of my agony came as a freshman when I lined up at center in practice. I was to hike the ball to a quarterback who was even smaller than me. Across the line was a *real* football player, who had a good twenty pounds on me. The ball reached the quarterback's hands. Without even slowing down, the nose guard knocked me over, and I toppled over the player I was assigned to protect. The sarcastic coach barked, "Nice tackle, Rose."

It's said that something good can come out of just about anything. I think I developed grit on the grass during those tedious, painful, exhausting days from August to November. What's more, I learned to move forward through disappointment, as I saw a typewritten *3* in front of my name each day at practice, indicating there were two others ahead of me in my position.

I sensed it was time to let my gridiron dreams go as my senior year approached. Dad helped me become an acceptable discus thrower, and the team was stretching for a workout. The track coach, who also led the football squad, pointed out that I missed the first team meeting. He asked if he assumed correctly that I wouldn't be going out for football the following year. I replied, "That's right," and he responded, "Okay." At sixteen, it was well established that I didn't have the tools of a gifted athlete. I figured the best way of letting go of something I wanted with all my heart was to learn how to not want it so much anymore. I chucked the discus a little over a hundred feet on my last throw, a personal record. Mediocre for high school, nowhere close to adequate for college. How was *I* special?

One way I fought awkward teenage years was by learning to juggle and ride a unicycle. These were things *I* could do, without a teacher or coach correcting me. Dad showed me the basic juggling pattern with three tennis balls, and to balance myself with one hand against our large freezer in the garage while pedaling the single wheel. As I improved through practice, I began thinking that this could be my path. Seeing me on my unicycle on the street in front of the house, a family friend called me *Andy the Clown*. The nickname proved to be prophetic. As an early teen, I obtained a brochure for Ringling Brothers and Barnum & Bailey Clown College. Just in case, I kept my academics at a marginally acceptable level. Ringling accepted applicants at seventeen, which I'd be after graduation. In my mind, I had proven myself ordinary. As a student. As an athlete. As an overall presence. The word *greatest* in the trademark, *The Greatest Show on Earth,* loomed in front of me. Perhaps, I thought, this was my turn.

I auditioned for Clown College in Fresno and sensed it had gone reasonably well. The most striking thing to me was seeing my greasepainted heroes up close. Boss clown Tommy Parish started things off by introducing himself. Only two other guys would be trying out with me. Both appeared to be in their thirties, long in the tooth for Clown College candidates. One of them could juggle some. By this time, I could juggle at a respectable level and manage to stay atop my unicycle. In addition to showing these skills, we were paired up to perform the old standard *More Pepper* gag. A couple of the clowns demonstrated it first. The sandwich salesman stops a customer. Foam rubber slices of bread, meat, tomato, cheese, and lettuce are as oversized as the colossal slab of ribs placed on the side of the car in *the Flintstones*. The salesman, with both hands, takes a similarly huge pepper shaker, and pretends to season the sandwich. The customer keeps asking for more. Finally, the customer sneezes loudly, and throws the entire sandwich in the air. The contents fall every which way, and the customer chases off the salesman.

Local media made an appearance, and I had the chance to mug for a TV camera. Tuba Heatherton, a journeyman clown, helped my improv. When the audition ended, Tuba said, "Come here, Rose," and kindly dispensed advice and encouragement. I had done what I could, and now it was time to get back to my life. And wait.

After the audition, I was in no hurry to return home and decided to bask in the circus atmosphere for a while. I wanted to milk every moment in this enchanted world before heading back to Modesto. Performers from the show had started to trickle in. A clown, not yet in greasepaint, was working his long-handled white juggling clubs. He was happy to chat. I recognized a kid about my age from the *King Charles Troupe,* which could best be described as the Harlem Globetrotters on unicycles. We talked shop a bit about riding on a single wheel. In the parking lot, I saw the clowns from the audition in jeans and tees, still sporting their greasepaint. I hid from them. I figured I had a successful audition and took care of my business. I didn't want to make a pest of myself.

I sauntered through the parking lot and recognized Elvin Bale's *Mechanical Monster,* a robotic serpentine apparatus that I'd seen the daredevil perform on at the Cow Palace in San Francisco. There was no hurry to get home. A more dedicated student would dash back to school to make sixth period. I wasn't one. I randomly picked Chowchilla as a turnoff for a lunch stop outdoors. I savored my fried chicken and coke with crushed ice in a large Styrofoam cup.

Life in the circus was still a distant dream. Until spring, I'd return to marking time.

When I felt lost in my adolescence, I found a missing piece of myself in my circus pursuits. This was something for me, apart from friends and family. Movies of this era also nurtured a sense of finding my own way. My mom, brother, sister, and I all cried while watching *Brian's Song.* In this true story, the character of football star Gale Sayers (played by Billy Dee Williams) announces to his teammates before a game, that his best friend, Brian Piccolo (played by James Caan), was stricken with cancer. At eleven years old I saw *Rocky,* with a central character who has a chance to redeem himself through his fists. On a date in high school, I saw

Flashdance, where Jennifer Beals' character has the grit to become a classical dancer, after working as a welder in Pittsburgh. The protagonists in these stories are loners, battling against forces that are resisting their success. Like them, my mind was set on becoming successful, one way or another. The circus would be my vehicle.

2.   ALMOST

The Carson & Barnes Circus came through Modesto on the same day as the prom. The dance didn't interest me. I was awkward and unpopular, just waiting to get out. San Francisco State University awaited, and I regarded it with dubious enthusiasm. What I really wanted, was to be in the circus. A boy can dream, can't he?

Carson & Barnes would be in town for a day. I found out where the big top was, on a lot behind Lou and Ted's Truck Stop. The springtime heat of Modesto lent itself to dreaming of something different. Mom let me borrow her Oldsmobile, a gold four-door. Charlie spent his last coin on a chance of winning a golden ticket to Willie Wonka's factory. Likewise, I ventured out to the huge tent, giving it one more shot.

The day at Carson & Barnes started out like it did at other shows where I pursued employment. I asked employees and was shuffled from one person to another. Getting nowhere, I eventually settled in to watch the matinee. A clown wielding a broom was comically sweeping the floor of the big top, meeting and greeting the audience. Our eyes met, and we exchanged a smile. He'd become my boss a couple weeks later. I found my place on the portable hardwood bleachers and took in the delights of the circus as always. Again, I gazed at the highly skilled performers in their dazzling costumes, wondering if they would become my colleagues.

I continued my sales call after the show and was eventually led to the proprietor, D.R. Miller. He was portly, with a craggy face and full head of grey hair. With his short sleeve white button-down shirt and dress slacks, Mr. Miller could have passed as one of the local retirees who poked around a circus lot. But his Oklahoma drawl, slow and thick as molasses, indicated he wasn't from these parts. We found a place to sit amongst the circus personnel's campers and RVs. After spending a lifetime in the circus, Mr. Miller could spot a kid who had it in his blood. I believe his initial attempt to discourage me was a test. Years later, I would learn in sales training that overcoming objections is a normal part of closing a deal. I wouldn't take no for an answer, maintaining that I could be a clown or juggle for him, whatever he needed. When Mr. Miller laid out the terms of seventy-five dollars a week, two meals a day, and coffee and sweet rolls in the morning, I knew I had it made. He jotted down names of the towns where the show would be in subsequent days. The circus would head north, with its final California stops in Redding and Yreka. I would eventually buy a one-way bus ticket to Grants Pass, Oregon. We shook hands, and I assured Mr. Miller that he wouldn't regret his decision. He mumbled something in response, and I got out of there. I had just talked myself into a job in the circus; I didn't want to risk talking myself out of one.

I drove home on Cloud Nine. Dad was at work. I asked Mom, "Remember when you told me that if I got offered a job in the circus, we'd talk?" Her jaw dropped and she said, "You got a job." She started crying. We waited for Dad to get home.

I greeted Dad in the driveway and proclaimed, "Send me my diploma." My parents cooled my jets somewhat. I had a couple weeks to wrap up school. Mom told me later that she gave me an out. I had time to ponder this adventure and could opt out if I wanted. Meanwhile, Dad did the sales job of his life, convincing my mother to let her seventeen-year-old child leave home, to a world none of us knew. Nothing would change my mind, though, and I was itching to go. Dutifully, I stuck around for graduation, feeling pangs of guilt that academically, I could have done much better.

I had the weekend to pack and tie up loose ends. Some friends of my family came by for a graduation party. I stuck around for a while in my three-piece, grey suit, bought for the occasion. It was a highly celebratory night for me, but not for the usual reason of a boy who had just graduated from high school. While I had failed to distinguish myself as a student, I felt that I was becoming outstanding in my own way, as a circus performer. My neighbors, brothers Bill and Jim, dropped by with some friends. I changed into a t-shirt and cutoff shorts. An ecstatic idiot, I piled them into the old white egg delivery van. Dad had granted me the privilege of driving it in my senior year. Far from a *chick mobile,* it was functional and got me around. My classmates and I made a couple stops at other students' parties. In all the awkwardness of adolescence, this was one instance when being a teenager felt right and true. In the sweet warm June night, I marveled at the world that lay ahead of me.

Before leaving on my adventure, my friend Judy dropped by the house, and we drove downtown to Graceada Park. The two of us sat on a bench in front of the Mancini Bowl, the band shell where my sister Lynne played the flute in summer concerts. We discussed our budding lives. Alas, she had a boyfriend.

Mom cried as she and Dad left me at the Greyhound station. It was an understatement to say that she'd been a good sport. Mom joked to friends that I'd be cleaning up after the elephants. We also laughed when a family acquaintance warned me to "stay away from the fat lady." Despite the jokes, my parents knew this would be a life-changing experience for their youngest child.

The bus rolled. I remember looking out the window as we passed Mount Shasta. There was a stop in Ashland, Oregon. Sometime before, my sister had attended the Shakespeare festival there. It gradually sunk in what I was doing, as I travelled mile after mile away from home. It thrilled me to see new towns from the window, though they were momentary glances. I probably slept some during the all-night ride.

An image of Stanford's heroic quarterback John Elway sticks in my head. The newspaper showed him that spring, blowing soap bubbles during the commencement ceremony. School ended for him too, and he would have his own adventure in the NFL.

In the morning, the bus arrived in Grants Pass. I could see the big top from the depot and decided to hoof it. It was about a mile, and I finally got there, clutching an army duffel bag in one hand and a small red trunk in the other. Mr. Miller spotted me and mentioned that I was out of breath. He sent me to the cookhouse to get something to eat. One or two people checked me out, making sure I wasn't a freeloader. I must have bolted something down.

I had no idea of what I was getting into. Maybe that was a good thing. I'd soon hear rumors of roustabouts who escaped the law and hooked up with the show. Supposedly, they would be out of town the next day, fugitives who would earn their keep by hauling up the big top. There was a rumor that one of them, who had only four lower teeth, had fled Cuba after killing members of his family. However, I found that most of the personnel at Carson & Barnes were kind and hardworking. The Mexican performing families would be particularly welcoming, as though I were one of their own. However, I'd find out that life on the road could be rough, and not everybody would look out for a boy of seventeen.

Geary Byrd, Mr. Miller's son-in-law, led me to my new digs. My living space was one of ten *sweat boxes,* closet-sized sleeping quarters in the back of a burgundy-colored diesel truck. I finally took it all in and absorbed the glorious Oregon summer day. I pulled out my clubs and started juggling to pass time. A local TV news reporter approached me. We chatted and I juggled a little for him. At Ringling, such a practice would be strictly verboten without a formal publicity appointment.

The show would usually set up in the middle of a field, with plenty of room to spread out the mobile city. The circus brass and veteran performers had RVs, and they would park alongside each other. An elderly couple also parked their rig there. The husband's job, as it were, was sitting in a lawn chair to catch any *towners* who might sneak under the tent. The rest of us, roustabouts, apprentice troupers, and families in rickety vehicles, were only allowed into the motor home community on official business. I knocked on one of the sheet metal doors, reporting to Barbara Byrd, Mr. Miller's daughter. She handed me a jar of cold cream to remove my grease-paint, joking that the girls would be following me around.

A skinny man in jeans and a t-shirt, seemingly in his thirties, approached me and asked if I was Andrew Rose. I responded, "Yes, sir." Scoffing at my formality, he introduced himself as the boss clown. He had long, dark hair, which was tied in the back.

There was nothing impressive about the features of my new boss. He talked with a slightly nasal tone. Small, dark eyes faintly reflected a mysterious anger. He provided an informal orientation to what would be my new workplace. The boss introduced me to another clown, his female roommate. With frizzy brown hair, she required no clown wig. Outside of greasepaint, she didn't bother with street make-up. Her features were plain. For a while, I would be welcome in their RV for official purposes, such as make-up instruction. In the trailer, I asked if either of them had thought about pursuing a career with Ringling. The boss said they were both *Ringling Brothers rejects*. His female counterpart added that they had a mutual *non*-admiration society with that organization. They had both entertained at Ringling Brothers and Barnum & Bailey's Circus World, a theme park north of Haines City, Florida. Eventually, the corporation would sell off the facility, and the park would fade away.

My new boss informed me that I would be worked into the matinee. I applied my make-up, and he said that it needed some work. I helped him carry props to *Clown Alley,* a section behind the bleachers, under the big top. We chatted and lugged various pieces of wooden and plastic equipment used in the ring for physical comedy. We walked through the midway, which featured two attractions. One was of giant rats, the other had exotic snakes. I visited Carson & Barnes years later and found that these displays had been discontinued. I can only guess how these animals were disposed of after the attractions were closed. I met and greeted circus patrons and served as assistant in the Levitation gag. A *swami* in an oversized purple, beaded turban puts another clown into a trance, covering him with a blanket from the neck down. The blanketed clown in a trance appears to levitate-into the air. But at the end, the *blow off* reveals the illusion. Two connected PVC pipes have clown shoes attached to them at the end. The clown under the blanket had been lifting his torso and the pipes at the same time, creating the appearance of floating. An old standard, but an effective one. Clown gags brought me back to the campfire skits we performed at Camp Jack Hazard in the Dardanelle mountains. If Carson & Barnes hadn't come along, I probably would have gone back as a staff member at the YMCA camp, where I had spent the previous summer.

My experience at Carson & Barnes seems as if it lasted a lifetime, though it was less than two months. We had no days off, performing twice a day. Wispy memories still fade in now and then, of a time when I *felt* more. Happier and sadder, with deeper intensity. Gradually I learned unwritten rules of my strange new world. Some with the show looked for angles to make an extra buck, no matter that one of those bilked was a naïve kid, freshly removed from his mother's apron strings. One joker in a polka dotted baseball hat got away with charging us a dollar a week under the table for connecting our lights in the sweat boxes where we lived. I figured it was not wise to fight that one.

Perspective for a teenager is difficult to maintain. It may have been even more of a challenge for me than most, as I made my way at seventeen through this strange society. I had sent off my Clown College application before leaving for Carson & Barnes. I figured it was my one shot at Ringling, the *big time,* as it were.

Roger Babson wrote that "the finest command of language is often shown by saying nothing." This is a notion I should have practiced. For those around me it was a job, a business. Young greenhorns like me got in the way. The foot juggler, struggling with English, told me to stop staring at him. I was a kid in a massive, tented candy store.

Every week or so, I'd find a pay phone and make a collect call to chat with my parents. A telephone operator showed her exasperation after asking me who was calling, and I responded, "the family clown."

3. SUMMER

The boss clown and I never hit it off, and I gravitated toward developing my own juggling routine. For a while I was clowning in the show, then taking off my greasepaint to perform my act. The boss eventually declared that I wasn't showing enough dedication and kicked me out of Clown Alley. Mr. Miller let me stick around, though I had to earn my keep by assisting the trapeze artists with their rigging.

The rigors of the road, being away from family, and sleep deprivation took their toll, but I reminded myself that I *was in the circus.* Days and weeks began to mount, and I fell into a routine. It was still dark when the surly horn of the repair truck roused us. I'd pull on my jeans and tee, which remained semi-clean at best until we'd reach another laundromat. I'd splash water on my face from the bucket outside my sweat box and stroll to the cookhouse for a prepackaged pastry. The starchy start of the day varied between donuts bathed in powdered sugar and cinnamon rolls.

I'd ride shotgun to the next town with a gregarious lady who went by Pebbles. Besides driving the sweat box truck, she served as a showgirl. We came to enjoy each other's company. We were never at a loss for words, as highways of the Northwest and Midwest provided scenery for our ongoing dialogue. I would often nap, the sun eventually greeted me, and I'd open my eyes to yet another freeway or two-lane road. Pebbles would shout, "Idaho," and we would rumble through a new state. On a short jump, we'd pull in while it was still early morning hours. The big rig gargled diesel fuel through its idling engine and eventually shut off.

There was rain occasionally, not just the mild showers that I'd experienced in Central California. Once we pulled into a lot and promptly got stuck. Pebbles yelled out the window, "Dewey, get me an elephant!" Our advance man, who could easily be cast as a Fuller brush salesman, arranged for a beast and harness to pull us out.

I had nothing to do until the big top was raised, so I'd head back to my sweat box for a nap, opening my door now and then to observe the massive tent being propped up by metal poles. Occasionally, the show set up in a parking lot; usually it was out in a field somewhere. When the tent was finally up, it was time for me to get to work. I wasn't adept at conceptualizing the labyrinth of cables, ropes, and winches that comprised the flying trapeze rigging. Nevertheless, I'd show up and do my best. Mexican trapeze artists, including my buddy Rafael, would bark commands in broken English to pull and loosen the cables. I half comprehended their instructions. Rafael derisively gave me the nickname *Charly,* after the mentally impaired character in the Cliff Robertson movie. I was often relegated to grunt work, hauling net poles and hammering stakes. I didn't mind too much, figuring that I had to earn my keep. Truly studying the mechanics of trapeze rigging would have been a good idea, but I wasn't interested. It was just a chore for me.

When the rigging was finally up, I rejoiced that the toughest part of my day was over. It was time to clean up and make it over to the cookhouse for lunch. The cookhouse line formed in a leisurely affair. We'd grab army trays and silverware, then get in line. Rib sticking fare loaded us up with necessary carbs for the day. Black-eyed peas became a familiar friend, along with a mixture of cubed potatoes and mixed vegetables. We sat *al fresco* under the cookhouse tent at yellow picnic tables that were never entirely clean. There was always a thin layer of transparent grease with a touch of gray. Each table had a bottle of squeezable Parkay on top. Frequently there would be an open loaf of *Texas Toast,* double-sliced white bread. There was regularly meat of some type, such as baked chicken or cubed beef in barbecue sauce. Once we were served fried catfish. The pecking order of performers and roustabouts disappeared at the cookhouse, where we shared the common interest of filling our bellies. It didn't take long to become nodding acquaintances with just about everybody there, as we would sit and gab freely.

For a seventeen-year-old boy, the priority of food outweighed camaraderie. Early on in my stay with Carson & Barnes, the perpetually ravenous monster of my teenage stomach got me in trouble with the cookhouse lady. The standard was to be limited to second helpings, but I was still hungry and more than willing to buck the system. It took some courage to approach the eternally sneering hash slinger with stringy black hair. Like a scene from *Oliver Twist,* she turned me away when I asked for more. The boss clown was still my superior at the time and reasoned that since I wasn't getting paid much, I should be amply fed. I give him credit for that one.

I boldly approached Geary Byrd. The proprietor's son-in-law held the title of *General Superintendent.* I figured he oversaw such matters. Geary agreed with my grievance, saying he threw away excess food every day. The next meal, I smiled in self-satisfaction at the serving wench in the cookhouse and received my third helping.

I would usually practice my juggling before the matinee. Carson & Barnes boasted a gimmick of five rings as opposed to three, a true example of quantity over quality. I was always able to find a free ring where nobody else was rehearsing. My bones, muscles, and tendons, still in development, gradually forged a partnership with the clubs, rings, and balls. I became adept enough to perform a decent act. Before long, jolly Ted, whose job with the show wasn't clear to me, would yell *"Doors! Doors!"* always twice. It was time to vacate the big top, freshen up with water from my bucket, and get ready for the show.

The circus parade around the big top floor was known as *spec,* short for *spectacle.* That, along with my juggling act, as it were, constituted my appearances in the show. The theme, as announced by ringmaster Barry Brazell, was *The Golden Age of Chivalry.* Barry and I would cross paths again during his short tenure as assistant performance director with Ringling Brothers. The easygoing red-headed ringmaster disguised his southern drawl and could introduce acts with the best of them. He was also the show's unofficial morale booster. Out of the audience's line of vision, Barry would perform such antics as ridiculously talking into his shoe like a phone while we made our way around the hippodrome track during spec. The two of us became friends as I'd chat with him in the tent between performances.

The seven day a week routine usually remained unbroken, as the sweet summer days and nights melted away. I had been a TV junkie as a kid but didn't seem to go through withdrawal once I was on the road. I kick myself for not reading more as a child, though I started up that summer. I found *Weedy Rough,* by Douglas C. Jones, along the way. The cover and title reflected my mindset. I figured it would focus on rural America, a small town like the ones I was sweeping through daily. I could relate to the misadventures of its main character, Duny Gene Pay. Like me, Duny Gene had his ups and downs as a teenage boy in the heartland. Also, at a gas station I picked up *Celebrity* by Thomas Thompson, a long-forgotten paperback about three boyhood friends who become a movie star, professional athlete, and evangelist. I had entered show business through its rectum. That book allowed me to dream, flipping through the pages on the filthy mattress of my aptly named sweat box. Walt, the grizzled mechanic, rhythmically ground out his smoker's hack next door. The circus program stated that he was a retired Air Force Colonel. My sweat box, in the weeks to come, would be little more than a place to sleep. The cool shade inside of the big top was my real home. The few weeks I spent at Carson & Barnes allowed me the opportunity to get a feel for the rhythm of the performance. I started as a circus fan and would never tire of sneaking a peak from behind the bleachers. Wiry, ten-year-old Armando would spill a bottle of water on the low wire, pretending to be drunk. He'd stagger to the song *Tequila,* and it was always fun to watch.

24

And then there was the flying trapeze. My buddy Lalo was just beginning to complete the triple somersault, and it was probably more exciting for us to watch than for the spectators because we were keenly aware of his day-to-day toil. I was also exposed to the harsh reality of the sport, seeing up close the fresh scrapes on his shoulders from sliding across the net after a miss. Rafael, who would become my best friend there, would let out a triumphant scream and *style* proudly to the audience after completing his trick and returning to the pedestal. I watched my friends perform on the rig twice daily, and thoughts crept up about becoming a catcher. A decade would pass before I'd climb up to the catcher's trapeze myself.

I also loved watching the trained animals but steered clear of them when I could. The area backstage would become crowded with horses. I was advised that these were the most dangerous of the circus animals. While tigers were always caged and elephants moved slowly, horses could kick a person who was nearby. Mr. Miller sat with a watchful eye in a lawn chair in front of the center ring and only got up to put a line of horses through their choreography when it was time. Despite his age and girth, he moved deftly while directing the equine routine, dressed in a tailored suit and cowboy hat. The elephant act had a Broadway theme, with the band blaring *New York, New York*. Showgirls wore smartly designed pink and black top hats and tails over fishnet stockings. I began to let myself think about getting to big cities like New York as a Ringling clown, but I knew there was no way to speed the plow. I'd have to wrap up my time at Carson & Barnes, and then, if accepted, perform at Clown College. Manhattan would come or it wouldn't, but for the time being, I enjoyed the familiarity of the show's music and displays, while I waited to go on. The same song would seemingly taunt me again when I did reach Clown College. One of the major showcases of our performance there blasted Frank Sinatra's version of New York, New York. Several members adept on stilts kick-stepped in formal wear. Long satin pants ran down the length of the stilts, giving the impression that they stood a story above us. My teenage mind took this literally, that they were a cut above. My roommate was chosen for that number, and I tried to be happy for him.

My time at Carson & Barnes gave me a real sense of what circus life was like, and I decided that I wanted more. I grew to love the daily grind. Then there would be the occasional event, a ripple in the sea of tranquility. A Franzen Brothers Circus promoter saw me work and offered me a job with a substantial raise. I took his phone number but didn't seriously consider calling him. One way or another, I knew that life would change, come fall. A career as a college student at San Francisco State would most likely begin, but the Clown College application that I had mailed in was still in the back of my mind. For now, I was in the circus. I reminded myself to enjoy it while I could.

Once the rigging was up, I remembered how lucky I was. Yet another day, I'd walk into the huge orange and blue striped tent, marveling that I was being paid to be there. Circus *civilians,* I found, wanted to talk to me, including reporters. We rarely found out if our picture had run in the local paper, because we'd be of town the next day. However, at the end of June, the show stayed for two days in Spokane, Washington. I'm smiling in newsprint, with a reasonably appealing clown face. Somehow, I'm identified in the photo as *Brian Woerle.* I never heard of anybody by that name.

At times it seemed like a small, simple, perfect world. It even had a dab of high culture. The brassy band of old pros showed their classical chops through playing *Rondeau* from "Symphonies and Fanfares for the King's Supper," by Jean-Joseph Mouret. I recognized it as the theme from PBS' *Masterpiece Theater.* A lovely niece of the circus proprietor would sing *If Ever I Would Leave You,* from *Camelot.* Spec during my second year with Ringling would have a similar theme, when we regaled the audience with *The Living Unicorn.* Even the blue and purple color scheme was the same, though the latter was exponentially more ornate. Still, I was never more content than when I'd sport my Robinhood costume at Carson & Barnes, stroll in my place, waving to yet another crowd we'd barnstorm.

Fortunately, I proved myself an adequate juggler after the boss clown dumped me. My buddy Alex, a trapeze flyer, gave me a beaded black costume. That, worn with a ruffled tuxedo shirt, provided a passing ensemble. From spec until the end of the evening performance, I lived like Micky Dolenz' character in the TV show *Circus Boy*.

Life was simple. Meals were provided at the cookhouse, and I'd practice my juggling and socialize in the big top between performances. The reality of manual labor would come with the tear down of the tent at night, as I helped dismantle the flying trapeze. I handled net poles and helped lower ropes threaded through pulleys. Mostly, sensing the mad dash to pack up the mighty beast, I tried to stay out of the way. One night, Bob, the drummer, wasn't pleased as I lowered a cable and it hit against a cymbal of his prized kit. I never tired of watching the harnessed elephant help in the process. The deft handler would wrap a chain around one of the massive stakes that were pounded into the hard earth. The other end of the chain was attached to the elephant's harness. Then the huge grey mound of flesh would raise its foot, plucking the yard-long piece of metal from the ground as if it were a toothpick. A couple hours later, the field would be empty again. We'd be awakened at dawn and move somewhere else.

The highlight of my day came twice when I would get to juggle for the audience. I was between rings four and five. Once or twice, I had to chop weeds to make a clearing so I could perform my act. Barry would announce, "an expert exhibition of manual dexterity." The arena was filled with jugglers, and we went to it. Overall, the juggling display was considered the weak link in the performance chain. When there was a need to shorten the show's length, juggling was cut. There would be nothing for me to do after spec, and I welcomed the escape.

This happened in Clinton, Iowa, where I changed from my Robinhood costume to stroll a while. Whether this was the stretch of asphalt that brought me in that morning or would lead my way out tomorrow, it didn't matter. Seemingly out of nowhere, a small stadium appeared, sporting the familiar orange and black logo of the San Francisco Giants baseball club. Nobody bothered me as I walked inside. I took a seat several rows up from home plate and watched a guy efficiently spray the dirt infield with a garden hose. Below, many young men a little older than me had pursued their own dreams and would continue to do so on this field. A handful would make it to the major league level. A decade later, I found myself sitting in a professor's office at California State University, Stanislaus, where I was pursuing a master's degree. On the wall, I noticed a baseball card from the Clinton Giants, with a picture of my instructor's son. I didn't bother telling him that I had once gazed upon this field.

But almost always, juggling was part of the show. When my act was over during the matinee, I'd close the small red theatrical trunk that held my props and place it in an unused area behind the big top bleachers. Then I'd wrap a bathrobe around my costume and head to the cookhouse for supper. It would have been just as easy to drop by my sweatbox, hang up my costume, and slip into a pair of shorts and t-shirt. Nevertheless, I had seen other performers attired like this backstage and wanted to show that I was one of them. There would be more time for practice before the evening performance. On these delightful afternoons, we would hone our skills and socialize.

The routine would infrequently be broken up in a larger town like Spokane, where we set up in a mall parking lot for two days instead of one. It was fun to be a city slicker for a while, and it also meant I wouldn't have to haul up or take down the trapeze rigging for a day. Sundays would also provide a respite, as the show would have a late morning and matinee performance bunched together. The tent would be packed up by twilight, and we would celebrate our weekly night off. I'd find someone to tag along with for pizza, a movie, bowling, whatever was around. Later on, D.R. Miller would host crap games in the cookhouse; all comers were invited to reinvest their money in the show. He would click a stack of quarters rhythmically, as performers and roustabouts alike tried their luck. The impromptu casino even had a green felt cloth, complete with necessary markings for shooting dice. Revenue for the show also came through beer sales. A captive audience gladly paid two dollars a can. I'd occasionally down a Stroh's or two; nobody bothered carding me. Eventually, the lights would go out and the only sound would be crickets.

So passed those sleepy summer days and nights, as we wended our way through one dusty lot after another. There was a dreamy continuum in this routine. Another town. Another set-up. Another languid practice session between shows.

When I was a kid and dreamed of this life, I recall Circus Vargas coming through Modesto, and I was old enough to attend alone. I preferred it that way. I got dropped off to watch a matinee. After the show, from a distance, I looked under the big top. A prop guy was messing around awkwardly on a unicycle. Looking on was a kid about my age, whom I recognized as a performer in the show, but now he wasn't sporting the smart costume from his family's acrobatic act. He was just a kid in cutoff jeans. There was a chance I would have gotten kicked out, had I sauntered into the tent to hang out and chat a while. Something told me if I did get ousted, it would shatter my perception of this seemingly perfect little world. I admired it from afar for a bit, then turned around to look for Mom's white and brown station wagon to pick me up. At Carson & Barnes I got to be that kid for a while.

If my circus adventure ended there, it would have been a worthwhile experience that I would always remember fondly. However, there would be more. A phone call would change my life. I had dutifully called home from the road, a practice I would continue throughout my travels. Strangely, one afternoon I received a message from Mom. Naturally, I was concerned and sought out the nearest pay phone. Before cell phones, it couldn't have been easy for Mom to contact a circus that moved daily. She told me that I had a message from Ron Severini, the Dean of Clown College. We had never met face to face, but I knew what he looked like from his picture in the Ringling program. I dialed the number. I visualized his handsome face and sympathetic brown eyes as we talked. Mr. Severini started off by asking me how I liked Carson & Barnes. I replied that it wasn't The Greatest Show on Earth, but that I was enjoying my summer there. He asked me if I wanted to be a clown. I replied that I wanted to be a *Ringling* clown. Finally, he said, "Okay, Andy," and the friendly chat culminated with an offer to attend the 1983 class. I hung up, realizing I was a step closer to fulfilling my young life's dream.

4. MATRICULATE

It was time to plan my trip home. I did what I needed to do at the Carson & Barnes Circus. My endeavor had apparently impressed the dean of Clown College enough to get me a place in the school.

I had been at Carson & Barnes through the latter half of June and all of July, long enough to become at least nodding acquaintances with most of the people there. Performers, men who hoisted and dismantled the tent, and concessionaires were known as *kinkers*, *big toppers*, and *candy butchers*, respectively. Various additional roustabouts rounded out the personnel. Come July's end, I was the talk of the town. *Jackpots*, rumors on the circus, were a mainstay for its employees. Whether true or not, those on the road loved to gossip. The rumor about me was true. Everyone I knew, and a dozen or so I didn't, congratulated me. When I arrived, I had come to the show in obscurity. I recall the awkwardness of strolling into the cookhouse for the first time, being asked if I was supposed to be there. Now everyone with the show knew about me and my Ringling aspiration. Almost thirty years later, my brother-in-law would make the brilliant pronouncement, "Magic spoken is magic broken." Perhaps I should have kept my admission to Clown College private, making a quiet exit from Carson & Barnes, but in my excitement, I couldn't wait to tell anybody who would listen.

My pal Donna, the showgirl, lived in the sweat box next door. Naturally, she was elated for me. Carlos offered me a spot with his family's acrobatic troupe, thinking that I now had a connection with the Greatest Show on Earth. He, his wife, and two school age children would train diligently between shows. His chubby toddler also joined in, somersaulting on the worn mat, already learning the family trade. They lived in a converted municipal bus.

It was still thrilling for me to be around the men and women in brightly spangled costumes while I waited to perform. As my mudshow days wound down, I reminded myself to treasure these times behind the big top bleachers. I could tell Mr. Miller was proud of me for sticking it out during the summer and displaying a strong work ethic. He stated that I'd be welcome back if not chosen for Ringling's Clown Alley.

But the boss clown failed to share such sentiments. If he sensed that I had talent, he wouldn't let on. The closest he could bring himself to encouragement was that I had a shot, being seventeen and white. He added that my ancestry could also be an asset, a reference to the Feld family, Ringling's owners, who were Jewish. I had heard about another veteran of Carson & Barnes who had grown up in a circus family and become an expert juggler. He had been accepted to Clown College some time before but hadn't been picked to go on the road. What's more, my friend Barry, the ringmaster, had gone to Clown College and didn't end up in Ringling's Clown Alley. After the initial rush of being accepted to the school, I realized there would be one more step to the big time.

I loved being at Carson & Barnes but recognized this adventure had run its course. There was a substantial price for maintaining my berth in the show. I never enjoyed bathing out of a plastic bucket and being awakened by a blaring horn from a repair truck at the 5 AM hour. And patience was continuing to wear thin with the trapeze artists that I helped, or hindered, with their rigging. Mom got me to admit on the phone that I was tired of this.

My parents, always incredibly supportive, flew to Minneapolis and rented a car to come out and see the show. The big top wasn't hard for them to find in Charles City, Iowa.

It was fun to watch the show with my folks before it was my turn to perform. When the time came for the juggling display, my buddy Rafael let me have the ring to myself during the matinee, knowing it would be my last day there. I'd joined up well after the season was underway and my area to perform was between rings four and five. I'd always remember Rafael's kindness for giving me his space in the ring on what was a truly special day for me. Naturally, I was excited to present in front of Mom and Dad. I set my props early in the ring, which would prove to be a foolhardy move. It was shortsighted to do this; a clown act came on before mine. The boss clown didn't like that. After the juggling act was over, he tersely stated that if I ever did that again, he would throw me out of the ring. I snapped back, "Oh, you try it."

That night, as usual, I used the limited space under the seats of the big top to warm up. The boss and I stared each other down, wordless. Then he screamed and dived in to tackle me. Instantly it registered that he was trying to bang my head against a tent pole. Instinctively I threw punches and heard a loud crack. Circus personnel backstage separated us as the fracas spilled out into the midway. A snow cone vendor gave the maniacal harlequin some shaved ice for his face. Through clown white and blood, a single brown eye seemed to bore through me. I never saw him again.

My friend Fernando was a stalwart circus veteran who could balance his entire body on an index finger. He quoted a Kenny Rogers' song, "Sometimes you have to fight to be a man." I pulled myself together and performed my act.

After the evening's performance, as always, I completed my chore of dismantling the trapeze rigging with the Flying Randalls. While tearing down, my friend Gloria called me aside. She was a versatile performer, as Barry introduced her as "the mistress of the swinging head balance." Gloria, whom I adored, said that she hoped I'd make it into Ringling Brothers, but if I didn't, she would like me to catch for a trapeze troupe she was putting together. I looked at her questioningly, having never caught anybody. She squeezed my arm and said, "You're pretty strong."

That night, I introduced Mom and Dad to people I met on my adventure. The cookhouse stayed open on Sunday nights to hawk beer and fry hamburgers. Mom, Dad, and I hung out a while, drank a Stroh's, and got caught up. Later would come the Sunday Night crap game ritual, where Mr. Miller would recoup some of his overhead from willing employees, but not from me. The cookhouse generator hiccupped, and for a few seconds, lights went out. There was darkness in the warm Iowa night. Mom, Dad, and I had a stark reminder of what happened during the last performance and figured it was best to get out of there for my safety.

The three of us drove off to Minneapolis, where we would spend the night. Our flight home wasn't until the following evening, so we had some time to kill there. I made Mom pose for a picture, throwing my hat in the air like Mary Tyler Moore. *The Mary Tyler Moore Show* was based in Minneapolis, and I figured this would be a pleasing symbolic gesture. Whether watching me under the big top in Charles City, Iowa, or my sister groveling as a cast member of a Greek tragedy at the University of California, Santa Cruz, open air theater, Mom and Dad were fanatically there to support us.

The next day Carson & Barnes would pull into Clear Lake, another town in Iowa. Rock and roll fans recognize Clear Lake as the town where Buddy Holly gave his last concert before dying in a plane crash. The show would play Cresco the following morning. After that would come the Wisconsin leg of the tour: Prairie du Chien, Platteville, Monroe, and Jefferson. They'd hit Baraboo, home of the Circus Hall of Fame, on August 13. That was as far as my route card went.

The tour had taken me through fifty-two towns in fifty-four days. I saw bits and pieces of Oregon, Washington State, Idaho (one day in Kellogg), Montana, Wyoming, South Dakota, and Iowa. Mainly, there were the common sights, the big top, the lot where it was set up, and my sweat box.

There's a tale about a circus dog that was tethered daily to a trailer and buried a bone in the dirt. The next day, on the next lot, he would try to dig it up.

5.   HOPE

I had a month to prepare. I'd daily practice applying my grease-paint and work on my juggling and unicycle riding. I knew the competition would be fierce. My parents would show empathy, but this was something I would have to go through alone. Mom and Dad tried to remind me that this experience was wonderful, in and of itself.

Meanwhile, I'd take advantage of every possible edge I could think of. I dropped by to see a Clown College audition at San Francisco's Cow Palace. I met the dean, Ron Severini, face-to-face. Fortunately, the black eye from my fracas with my boss at Carson & Barnes had faded. I made plans to attend the big show in Oakland. Mr. Severini had recommended I ask backstage, and the boss clown, Wayne Sidley, would be happy to show me around. It thrilled me to think that I could be a part of this organization.

I sat in the audience and watched the clowns go through their choreography in the opening number. My vantage point was in the upper deck, off to the side of Ring 3. Some fifty yards away, a group of eight clowns stepped in time with the music. They easily sauntered to the band's cheerful blare. Outlandish combinations of red, pink, and purple were sported in the opening production number. They were entirely encrusted with sequins and rhine-stones. "Someday," I murmured to myself.

I knew that with success at Clown College, *someday* could very well arrive. During intermission, I waited to be introduced around Clown Alley by the boss clown. As I anticipated entrance into the inner sanctum of buffoonery, a gregarious female security guard chatted me up. I told her what I was up to, and she responded, "Baby, you lookin' *good*. Why you wanna be a clown?" I wasn't in much of a mood to talk about myself and decided to turn the tables. I made small talk by asking if she knew any of the Warriors, Oakland's professional basketball team. Finally, the boss clown greeted me cordially and showed me around. I tried to keep cool while shaking hands with my idols. Last year I was asking the clowns for autographs.

Clown Alley had the air of relaxed efficiency. Oakland, to the traveling troupe, was just another city on the road. Steamer trunks and folding chairs filled the room. Some of the clowns were sitting at their stations. Everyone was cordial and knew why I was there, including Tim Holst, the performance director. Mr. Holst kindly stated that he hoped to see me on the road.

The biggest thrill of the day was making the acquaintance of Lou Jacobs, the iconic master clown who would ultimately spend sixty-two years in Ringling's Clown Alley. The sweet man, eighty years old, referred to my long, wavy hair (this was a long time ago), joking that I didn't need a wig. I felt like an insider as I got to see him without the iconic cone-shaped clown head that he was famous for.

I returned home from my field trip and continued with my self-written Clown College prep course. During my summer at Carson & Barnes I had learned a few tricks of the trade. For instance, soap and water won't remove a properly applied clown make-up, which is dried into a paste with baby powder. Instead, the wondrous Suave Baby Shampoo miraculously cut through the greasepaint. I would put on my clown face first thing and then remove it while showering. I'd then practice my skills diligently. Warm days of late summer gave me the opportunity to juggle on the back lawn. I'd also borrow Mom's car and drive to the parking lot of Stanislaus Elementary School, which I had attended from ages six to eleven. While faculty was still enjoying summer vacation, I had the asphalt to myself. I used the large, paved surface to practice my unicycle riding. Few cars drove by on Kiernan Avenue to break my concentration; the facility was then tucked between peach orchards. It was fitting that I gravitated toward the old *jail,* as we sardonically called it. As a child there my dreams were endless, and they appeared that way again.

I knew that arena choreography would be part of the program, so I enrolled in dance lessons. I also rested and waited. I didn't socialize a lot, feeling the need to wrap my mind around the upcoming task. At seventeen the magnitude of this endeavor bore down on me.

Already I had beaten the odds. Nobody expected me to be hired with a circus out of high school. I had subsequently earned a berth at Clown College. Still, there was one final hurdle. Days ticked slowly.

Despite my fear, it felt good to *want* something so much. Until now, languishing in high school, my days had been largely spent wallowing in a haze of mediocrity. I got by, lacking passion. At the beginning of the semester, a zealous sophomore composition teacher likened us to a collection of racehorses. He predicted that there would be those among us listed as *also ran,* trotting along without achieving excellence. I was in that group. This time would be different. I refused to reduce myself to obscurity.

My roundtrip ticket to Venice, Florida, home of Ringling's winter quarters and Clown College, was bought. My list for items to bring was checked and rechecked. All I needed was for the nine-week test to begin. Would I emerge triumphant?

I was about twelve when I saw *Dirty Harry* on TV. In an early scene, Harry (Clint Eastwood) finds a perpetrator lying on the sidewalk, unable to get away. Anyone who's a seventies film buff is familiar with Eastwood's speech while pointing a .44 Magnum, which can "blow your head clean off." Harry proclaims that in all the confusion, he lost track of whether he spent all the rounds or if there was one left. The man on the pavement, figuring there's little to lose, proclaims, "I gots to know." Harry pulls the trigger, there's an audible *click,* and then he laughs. I knew that this was a once in a lifetime chance. *I gots to know.*

6. FALLING

It was a long day on jumbo jets. Then a tiny plane took me on the short jump from Sarasota, Florida to Venice. From there I caught a shuttle to the Kent Hotel, the quarters which we would dub Kamp Kent. I arrived in early evening. The hotel was located on the *Tamiami Trail,* a stretch of highway that extended from Tampa to Miami. Most of the students would be staying across town at the more ornate Venice Villas, a vacation spot by the beach for middle class visitors to Florida's gulf coast. One or two students would complain that we were secluded from the female clown hopefuls, but overall, none of us at the Kent seemed to mind much. We weren't in resort mode.

Some of the guys had gathered on the breezeway in front of the lobby. There wasn't a sense of competition…yet. When the van dropped me off and I saw among them a dwarf, I figured I was in the right place. There was also longhaired, skinny Charlie, making his juggling clubs dance. He'd make money by sewing and selling fellow students parachute pants in his spare time. Charlie also encouraged the class members to sign his white VW bus with a black marker. Phil, always amiable, was also there. He was older and more self-assured, with an engineering degree under his belt. Motherly Ann, owner of the Kent Hotel, eventually arrived. We started calling her *Mom,* which stuck. She gave us a rundown on the place, how the food in the coffee shop was cheap and good. Phil said he could use a cup of coffee, and a small group of us gathered at a table. My teenage metabolism signaled, as always, the need for food. I chomped heartily on a hot roast beef sandwich with mashed potatoes and gravy.

Eventually, my roommate Brent arrived and introduced himself. He turned up from St. Peters, Missouri, thirty miles outside of St. Louis, but he looked like a surfer, handsome, blonde, lean, and confident. He and I shared an average size motel room, comfortable enough.

Our living quarters were serviceable. There was a TV for distraction. A sliding glass door led to the central grounds. Ann let us know that clean white towels would be provided but we were not to use them to remove our greasepaint. I would absentmindedly break this rule one evening and selfishly blame Brent when she asked. A small kitchen was to be shared with Jim and Robb, other would-be clowns in the adjoining room. It was comfortable enough. All of us knew why we were there. The tiny lobby had a stack of Circus World brochures as a reminder, but we didn't need it. It was autumn, but the balmy Florida air signaled that I was away from the familiarity of home. We eventually turned in, and Brent asked me if I attended church.

Morning came, and the bus arrived, already loaded with the students from the Venice Villas. The white bus had *Ringling Brothers and Barnum & Bailey Clown College* painted in caps on the side. The letters in *CLOWN COLLEGE* were comically red, bulky, and tilted. I imagined the townspeople of Venice looked forward to seeing the bus as we were shuttled from our living quarters to the arena, giving identify to their town. For us, it was a prison transport of sorts, albeit one where we were willing captives. For nine weeks, we'd be shut out of society as Clown College students, but we were also locked out of the show unless we could prove ourselves worthy. Jeff, a slightly built southerner, had been a clown on the road and now served on the faculty. He would also drive the bus. Jeff displayed a calmness and grace that I wished I had. It was a ten-minute drive to the arena, the winter quarters of the Ringling Brothers and Barnum & Bailey Circus. I wanted to have a moment to myself to take it all in. That wasn't an option. Fifty-nine others were picked for the class. They were there for the same reason as I was.

Mr. Severini and I recognized each other from when I had attended the audition in San Francisco. I felt a little less intimidated as we exchanged greetings.

Clown College 1983 was underway. The school had started in 1968, after Irvin Feld bought the Ringling Brothers and Barnum & Bailey Circus for eight million dollars. Most of the clowns at that time were over fifty years old. The running joke was that these clowns could still fall over but not necessarily get back up again. There would ultimately be more than a thousand graduates from the school.

Mr. Feld launched two touring venues, the *Red Unit* and *Blue Unit.* Clown College would be held in autumn, finishing in time to replace clowns that were needed each season for both units. One shot, and we all knew it.

We gathered, and Mr. Severini broke the ice by announcing the combined weight of all of us altogether, a ridiculously high number in the thousands. He knew to keep this introduction light. There was no need to proclaim the obvious, that we were all thrown in a state of direct competition with each other. I assume at this moment we all looked around, wondering who would ultimately be chosen. Mr. Severini also listed jobs that students were leaving to attend the school. He mentioned *juggler,* and I wondered if that was me.

It was time to size up the competition. Mr. Severini called the names in alphabetical order, to introduce ourselves to the class. Brent's turn came early, and he spoke with sincerity. Frank simply held up his right fist, declaring he was from Brooklyn. An obviously jetlagged David simply stated that he was very tired.

Both Frank and David would be dismissed from the class. I would catch up with Frank backstage in New York, during my second year on the road. He was still hurt and bewildered about being sent home early. Frank related to me that he was called out of class, asked to bring his personal effects with him, and that was that.

More students would eventually leave, along with the rumors of why, trailing behind them. One aspiring clown supposedly exited Clown College after discovering she was pregnant. This rumor was substantiated some months later when she would bring her infant to the show.

I pensively waited my turn to introduce myself to the class. Phil simply clapped his hands like an encouraging coach and said, "Let's have a lot of fun." Robb made some remark that caused Mr. Severini to mockingly pretend that he was drawing a large check mark next to his name. R in Rose is toward the end of the alphabet, so I had time to think about my introduction. I figured to play it straight this time. "Everybody wants to be with the greatest, which is why I want to be in the Greatest Show on Earth." Mr. Severini smiled and had a knowing twinkle in his deep brown eyes. I had completed my first task.

A few more were to make their presence known. Karen announced that she was the oldest, at twenty-eight. She maintained her openness to providing sage advice. Frankie, the dwarf I met the night before, smiled and said in an exaggerated New York accent, "I'm from thoity-thoid and thoid." Toward the end was the ever-dramatic Mark, who blurted out that he was a big Lucille Ball fan. He repeated the song line from the Broadway play, *A Chorus Line,* "I hope I get it." Mark spoke for all of us.

A few days later, individual students were called in to meet with Irvin Feld. This would be a shot in the arm for me. Arnold Bramow, the Director of Special Projects, was also in the room. He had traumatically been shot in Washington, D.C., and was now in a wheelchair. Arnold would become a familiar face around Clown College and was always encouraging.

It was easy to talk to Mr. Feld, though meeting him face-to-face felt surreal. I had grown accustomed to seeing Irvin Feld repeatedly in his TV commercial for United Airlines. He would open a briefcase on a plane, and fake snakes would spring out of it. The commercial would close with Mr. Feld proclaiming that he was "working with a bunch of clowns."

We settled in and he asked if I had a girlfriend. Naturally, this was a strange question for a job interview. I presume Mr. Feld was screening candidates for the possibility of leaving the show for personal reasons during the yearlong tour. We transitioned to a discussion of my summer with Carson & Barnes. I explained my somewhat complicated situation of starting as a clown but finishing with a juggling act because I didn't get along with my boss. I caught myself short of talking about our fistfight. I was asked the boss clown's name, mentioned it, and Arnold said he remembered him.

Mr. Feld was highly encouraging and stated that "I would like to see you with us." I left the meeting elated, but the following weeks would be hard.

Instead of propelling my rousing start with the show's owner to a state of relaxed confidence, I became the proverbial bull in a China shop. Psyching myself out, I lived with a voice inside telling me that this was my job to lose. Daily, a battery of self-doubting questions would race through my still adolescent head: Why was I chosen to be here? What could I have done better? Do they notice the way I'm pigeon-toed? Do they care that I'm pigeon-toed? Do I carry my body too awkwardly? Did I upset somebody today? Did I dazzle somebody today? Did I lose my temper while rehearsing? Did somebody notice me losing my temper while rehearsing? Morning, noon, and night, I felt obligated to impress somebody. And there was the coursework. Despite my anxiety, I knew I had to laugh, fall, and tumble with the best of them. Then, in the evening, I lived in fear that one of the three with whom I shared living quarters would report to Mr. Severini that I did something unsuitable.

Mr. Severini had encouraged us to submit comedic ideas in the suggestion box. In his usual friendly manner, he advised us to "keep those cards and letters coming." Stamps of approval trickled in, to the delight of other students. My ideas were invariably met with a coldly signed, "NO, R.S.," the dean's initials denying one notion after another.

I figured it was better to keep submitting ideas, despite the fear of rejection. I also approached Frosty, who had a makeshift office in the back of Clown Alley. Glen "Frosty" Little, always kind and encouraging, was the executive director of clowns. He was pulled from performing on the road with the Blue Unit of the circus to instruct at Clown College. I walked to his desk and explained an idea in earnest. Although Frosty rejected the idea, our eyes met and he proclaimed, "You're thinkin'." I gnawed on the encouragement, exiting promptly from the unimpressive room with the concrete floor. I wanted to stay, but still couldn't. As students, we knew that Clown Alley would be our workplace, if chosen. A small wooden sign on the wall indicated that this was the alley of *the greatest clowns on earth*. Hopefuls were only allowed into the sacred space on official business.

Lou Jacobs was also brought in from the tour, dropping by to instruct us on comedic techniques. Seeing him reminded me that, no matter what the result, Clown College was truly a special, unique place. As I diligently worked the gritty polish into the silver-plated sousaphone to play in the clown marching band, Mr. Jacobs quipped that it was "shiny as a monkey's a#%." I assumed this was a compliment, much needed as I slogged my way through this strange school.

In high school social studies, we saw a film installment or two from John F. Kennedy's *Profiles in Courage*. At the end of the dramatic study of some great patriot, Kennedy proclaims in his familiar New England brogue that each man must find courage on his own. I learned to live with the daily obsessions of Clown College. They were accepted as part of my burden, as much as the gnats that would pester us in the arena. In my mind, Clown College was one big nail, and I was the hammer.

There was a small lending library, but I wasn't interested. My only exposure to it was when I was flipping through a volume on circus freaks, while waiting to establish my personal account for expenses in the office. The beginning of the book proclaims, *He loves us all.* Numerous fuzzy black and white photos compose the volume, people who made a living from their deformities in sideshows. I recognized *JoJo the Dogfaced Boy* and *The Bearded Lady.* Attractions new to me also caught my eye, including a man with an extra pair of arms growing out of his torso.

Terry, a fellow student, related that he had checked out a book on method acting by Stanislavski. I would have done well to study that book. Throughout the day and into the evening, I was expected to conduct myself as a clown, whatever that meant. As it turned out, Terry also had a stint with Carson & Barnes. He and I talked briefly about this experience, but at the time it seemed that both of us had bigger fish to fry. What's more, I wasn't too keen on others finding out about the run-in with my boss over there. Peggy Williams, the Assistant Performance Director for the Blue Unit, visited Clown College one afternoon. She was a Clown Alley veteran, and had worked with Maudie Flippen, a clown who ended up at Carson & Barnes. Maudie had held my hand and calmed me after my fight, as I prepared to perform my act. Terry introduced himself to Ms. Williams, mentioning their mutual colleague from the mudshow. I didn't dare.

Fear became a way of life, which I attempted to alleviate through calls home. Mom tried to comfort me. In a letter, she explained that at my age it was typical to have a lack of self-confidence. Back home, one of our favorite things to do had been to watch *The Odd Couple* together. For whatever reason, Oscar (Jack Klugman) relates to Felix (Tony Randall) that he asked his father, when he was a kid, for a toy train set. Oscar says he told his dad that if he got that train set, he'd never ask for anything again. I wondered if God, at the end of these nine weeks, would provide me with a contract in the Greatest Show on Earth.

Brent was a year older and several years wiser. I envied his sense of faith and perspective. He related that he didn't know what God had in store for him. Perhaps, Brent stated, he would go on the road with Ringling, or maybe "he just meant for me to go to Clown College."

44

I tried to convince myself that I came to this school with an advantage, a few weeks of Carson & Barnes under my belt. While there, although I had my falling out with the boss clown, I had picked his brain as a Clown College alumnus. Moreover, after coming home from the mudshow, I diligently practiced my make-up, juggling, and unicycle riding. This would be a job tailor-made for me. How dare anybody take it away? But doubtlessly other attendees felt the same way. As an exception, one guy, Keith, supposedly told Mr. Severini that he wasn't interested in going on the road.

In the movie *Chariots of Fire,* English sprinter Harold Abrahams proclaims that he has "only ten seconds to justify my whole bloody existence." I had nine weeks. If I wasn't one of *the Chosen,* it wouldn't be the end of the world, but you can't tell that to a teenager. At times I wondered how my life would have been different if I wasn't picked to tour with Ringling. I like to think that it would have built character. Then again, would I have let it destroy my life at eighteen years old?

Circus Vargas, the Franzen Brothers Circus, the No-Elephant Circus, and others were always on the lookout for Clown College graduates, and a number of students joined these and other venues. *The Modesto Bee,* my local paper, did a story about me. I told the reporter that if I wasn't chosen to go on the road, I would pursue a college degree. However, I maintained, it wouldn't be as much fun. Win or lose, I knew that I had to stick this thing out.

A handful of movie nights in the facility made for a calming salve. The arena's commissary, designed for the show's workers during the rehearsal period, served as a temporary theater. I admired the curtains with the Ringling logo. Naturally, we saw The Greatest Show on Earth. Jimmy Stewart co-starred, playing a clown who was evading the law after murdering his wife. I would always wonder how the story line made it past Ringling's public relations people. Such evenings eased the tension, but it was still present. I believe that it was after seeing Limelight, with Charlie Chaplin, that I thought out loud to another student, "Maybe I wasn't cut out to be a clown."

I invariably heaved a sigh of relief when we piled into the bus to go home. On Saturdays, Terry would lead us in the chorus from Sam Cooke's song: *Another Saturday night and I ain't got nobody…* A handful of students, like him, made it all look effortless. The gregarious southern beanpole appeared naturally made for the job as clown. Somehow a hearse had become his mode of transportation, and I rode once or twice with others in the back. I had both admiration and envy for him.

I'd get back to the hotel on Saturday night, and the next thirty-six hours would be mine. I'd remove my make-up in the shower and feel somewhat human again. Like *normal people,* Clown College students had Sundays to rest. However, they weren't particularly restful. We'd merely mark time under the balmy Florida sky. The Venice Villas were a stroll away, and students would frequently gather around the pool. With a little trawling, I'd initiate an impromptu therapy session with one of the older students. I'd ask how they dealt with the pressure. One of the female prospective clowns replied, "I cry a lot."

During one of my angst-ridden calls home, I had to ask for money. I had absentmindedly locked a fellow student's key in his room and had to pay for a locksmith. I didn't dare dispute the relative fairness of picking up the entire tab for fear that they would report me to Mr. Severini. The fellow prospective clown, a big guy with glasses, lectured me on responsibility. He was sent home early; rumor had it the student tested positive for amphetamines.

A somber John McKay, coach of the hapless Tampa Bay Buccaneers, somehow appeared to commiserate through a local TV station. I'd catch his weekly talk show, as he would sheepishly recap another loss. Weeks progressed, and he resorted to gallows humor. He once explained that his team had found new, creative ways of losing.

Ann, our landlady/mother figure, had some of us over to her house one afternoon to watch videos. Sometimes on Sundays I'd walk along the beach and search among the rocks for shark's teeth.

In 1977 I enjoyed a short-lived sitcom starring Greg Evigan and Paul Shaffer called *A Year at the Top*. Its premise was that two musicians, Greg and Paul, had signed a pact with the devil. The devil promises them a year of fame and fortune, and then he gets both of their souls. The devil never paid me a visit at Clown College. Nevertheless, it scares me to ponder what I would have been tempted to do if I had been approached the same way that Greg and Paul were.

Many years later, I'd become fanatically drawn to the opera *Turandot*. A young prince from a foreign land, Calaf, falls for Princess Turandot. Numerous suitors fail to answer the three riddles the princess asks and are abruptly beheaded. Calaf, however, proclaims that his love for the princess is more important to him than life itself. What were *my* three riddles, and how would I answer them? Each morning I awakened, Brent was still sleeping, and I wondered if Lady Ringling would be pleased with my antics.

I wasn't alone in these sentiments. Henry Ringling North wrote the following in *The Circus Kings: Our Ringling Family Story*: "The circus is a jealous wench. Indeed, that is an understatement. She is a ravening hag who sucks your vitality as a vampire drinks blood - who kills the brightest stars in her crown and will allow no private life for those who serve her; wrecking their homes, ruining their bodies, and destroying the happiness of their loved ones by her insatiable demands. She is all of these things, and yet, I love her as I love nothing else on earth."

As I write this, I forgive myself such fanaticism as a teenager. Nobody could have expected me to have, under these circumstances, a healthy perspective on the Ringling machine.

We bonded as a group at Clown College. I believe that it was more out of necessity than anything else. We were warned about the *Red Tide*. Harmful algae appeared in the Gulf of Mexico that fall, which caused the fish to die and be washed ashore. Thus, we were instructed to stay out of the ocean. An ever-jovial Terry organized the *Red Tide Pool Party* at the Venice Villas. The highlight was when he came out with a platter of tuna with red food coloring added, creating a sort of metallic hot pink hue. We ritually dipped in and shared a taste of the ghastly concoction.

Days ticked slowly and I was filled with both hope and dread. I didn't know whether I was already disqualified or not. Perhaps, I reasoned, I was written off the moment I swung a prop behind me and accidently hit Frankie the dwarf. He required seven stitches on his chin. I wanted to go home. I had no idea whether I was a frontrunner or also-ran, but one way or another, I had to finish this strange race.

Wednesday, October 5, 1983, was a week before my eighteenth birthday. From my scrapbook, there's a clipping from the *Venice Gondolier,* the local newspaper. By now, the rigors of Clown College were full on. Frozen in gray, twelve of us, ten boys and two girls, watch pensively as the instructor gives guidance. The picture from the paper has the following caption:

Under the "big top."

Then the article says the following:

> "Prospective clowns from around the country are taking courses ranging from acrobatics to stilt walking during the nine-week session of Clown College in Venice. Here, students at the only school of its kind in the country are learning "gags," or comic routines."

Ordinarily I would have been delighted to have my picture in the paper, but this time it didn't matter to me. My sole objective was to be hired. Of the twelve of us in the photo, five ended up on the road with Ringling.

Terry, Bob, Aaron, Sue, Mike, Laurie, Kevin, Jim, Steve, Andy, Mark, Mike (another one). All of us had put ourselves on the line, with hopes of achieving Ringling glory. One of the gatekeepers, an instructor named Jim Vogelgesang, is in the photo. Jim was, by then, a seasoned Clown Alley veteran. He's not in greasepaint, but the rest of us are.

48

The most ironic feature in this picture is that none of us are smiling. The photo is a faint reminder of Red Skelton's paintings of clowns. Much later, I was stricken by his work while making the transition to life *on the outside,* after leaving Ringling. I strolled on a Sunday evening with someone on San Francisco's Fisherman's Wharf. We walked into an art gallery that featured Skelton's paintings. The white foundation and colors of the greasepaint are finely crafted; it's easy to see Skelton's gift as a painter as well as comedian. But on closer look, all the clowns had a faintly sad, weary look in their eyes. The photo shows our faces in a similar way. We're sitting on the hard ring curb, our butts reminding us why we are there. Those ultimately chosen for the road would perform inside of this ring, to audiences of thousands. Looking closely, anyone can tell that it's hard for us to get comfortable. But as Karl Malden, who plays the warden in *The Birdman of Alcatraz* describes the prison to Burt Lancaster, playing the title role, "It isn't designed for comfort." This image reminds me of how the minutes crept by so slowly during instructional sessions. Ironically, there wasn't a lot of *clowning around.* That was, until we were called upon to do so. This was the essence of Clown College, learning to turn our funny bones on and off like a Pavlovian light switch.

It was hard to be funny under those circumstances. In a larger context, there were three other groups of students, receiving instruction in a rotation throughout the arena. Dance, juggling, and stilt walking were all part of the curriculum. The Class of 1983 was Ringling's sixteenth. By now, the *clown factory* was a well-oiled one. All of us in the photo are watching the instructor so intently, because we would inevitably get the chance to display to the rest of the group what we learned from him.

I look at that tense boy in the picture and am reminded of what I went through during those humid, fearful days. It comforts me that this pressure cooker is long buried in my past. I'm hunched over on the ring curb, sporting an *auguste* make-up, white around the eyes and mouth, while the rest of my face is flesh colored.

Peggy King and Tammy Parish, two veteran clowns teaching at my Clown College, would later pull me aside with an idea to design my new clown face. Peggy said that it would bring out my *boyish charm*. From that time forward I was a *white face* clown, with pink cheeks and black freckles.

In the photo, I wear shorts and a t-shirt. I appear to be uncomfortably rolling my ankles, trying to keep my pigeon-toed feet comfortable. I could scarcely imagine somebody telling me that I have nine weeks to write a book in its entirety, without the possibility to go back for editing. But as the photo shows, figuratively and literally, I didn't have a cushion. In Clown College there would be no edits or rewrites.

I recognized by the time the photo was taken, that I would have to ride it out, for better or for worse. The picture isn't one of clownish joy. It appears that all of us, in that moment, would like to be anywhere else but there. If a collective thought bubble were to be placed over our heads, it would say, "I WANT TO GO HOME!" Some of us, back to our jobs. Some of us, back to college (*real* college). Some of us, back to our parents. All of us were stepping away from our young lives for two months. It was a shot for what was, at that time, the holy grail of the circus world. We knew that most of us wouldn't grasp the sacred chalice when the course was over.

7. WRAP

Clown College would culminate with a gala performance, presented at the far end of the arena to the Ringling brass and other dignitaries, along with friends and family who were invited. As potential clowns, we would be identified by white canvas circles, marked with black numbers, safety pinned to our costumes. I would be number thirty-five. This was a tangible reminder that every move we made would be scrutinized, examined for the brass to evaluate.

The *coursework,* as it were, ended without fanfare. I think all of us were somewhat saddened that the majority wouldn't be going on the road. Students helped with odds and ends in the facility, while trying to stay out of the way. Win or lose, we obtained some semblance of closure while arranging the circus arena for the upcoming gala performance. There was a lot of standing around in this process, but none of us dared stray from our relegated places on the green rubber floor.

Just a short time longer to show how talented, wonderful, and perfect I was. Or wasn't.

I believe Clown College helped me deal with stressful instances later in life. Since then, I have yet to face in my mind such an *all or nothing* proposition. In higher education there was always another exam or term paper offering a chance for redemption. During my stint selling radio commercials, I frequently rejoiced in the fact that there would always be another business to call on if someone didn't buy. However, in this case, I would forever have been chosen as a Ringling clown. Or I wouldn't.

Students didn't receive report cards at the end of Clown College, only notification if we were accepted to go on the road. On the day of the gala performance, I met with Sandy Severini, the dean's wife, to close out official business. From my chair, I tried to scan the giant chart in the office, rating our skills. Mrs. Severini could tell what I was doing and asked if I was okay. I replied, "I'm a little keyed up about tonight."

Later, the bus would bring us back to Kamp Kent. Mom and Dad arrived, in addition to family members of other clown hopefuls. Some weeks before, a Ringling official announced that the gala performance would be the *icing on the cake,* a mere final deciding factor on those that would and would not be chosen to go on the road. Naturally, we speculated amongst each other, and it was theorized that the decision had already been made long before our show. Hence, we knew that most of us in the performance would be there as a mere formality, destined to be sent packing for good the next morning.

Mom, Dad, and I had the chance to spend some time together before the bus was to take us to the arena. We had a late lunch and talked. We embraced, and then it was time for me to go. I felt like Gary Cooper, waiting for the train of bad guys to arrive in *High Noon.* Mom looked into my eyes and said, "You wish it was over, don't you?" She handed me a greeting card. On the envelope was simply written, *#35.* I opened the card to find a drawing of a small harlequin, with the caption, *You are a star.* Mom wrote, "This says it all."

Typically, we'd arrive at the arena in the morning to put on our greasepaint. Then would come our daily training. However, this time it was different. All that was left was the performance. The bus rolled in, accompanying a typically warm Florida twilight. I tried not to think how pleasing it would be to laze around, stroll along the beach, or perhaps catch a movie in my room. But I knew my task. It felt like a long walk to the area relegated for us to apply our make-up. Along with the other students, I pulled my brown cardboard make-up kit from the shelf. In my nervousness some weeks before, I had let the contents get messy. Mr. Severini spotted this and admonished me. It didn't happen again. This time the box had a typewritten note inside. It was from Tim Holst, an encouraging message to us as Clown Alley hopefuls. Its greeting read "Dear

Joey." *Joeys* are the clowns, in circus jargon. Mr. Holst, performance director of the Red Unit, provided an inspiring message, closing it, "Go for it. Always."

There was no hurry to complete my clown face. I applied the white foundation with painstaking care, along with my other solemn classmates. It was well practiced by now. Make sure to get the front and back with the clown white. Pat slightly with the fingertips, to make the white even. Blend red on the cheeks, to make them pink. Scrape spaces away from my eyebrows, mouth, and nose with a Q-Tip. Go outside and douse my face with Johnson's Baby Powder (only that brand worked properly), bringing a portable mirror with me. Take a barber's brush and use it carefully, letting the white form a dry poultice. Then a red nose and mouth, with a little more powder. Finally, black eyebrows and freckles for my cheeks. Once with an eyebrow pencil, then, gently and slowly paint over with black. A touch more powder, and it was finished.

We donned our costumes and collected in the arena. Mr. Severini proclaimed that we were going to give the best #%& @*&# show these people had ever seen. There was a deafening collective cheer.

The gala performance seemed to go well enough. I forgot that I would be part of the *meet and greet* contingent, handing out popcorn to the audience. I had to let it go, hoping that nobody noticed. The wife of the venerable clown Lou Jacobs wished us well behind the curtain, acknowledging that it was a big night.

Nobody wanted a contract more than I did, but wanting it wasn't enough. I had to perform.

I managed to juggle well enough and stay on my unicycle. I was on my mark in the minor role I played in the gags I was chosen for. Soon it was time for the curtain call. The prelude was another appearance by the half dozen that Bunni the dance teacher chose as thematic dancers. I wasn't one of them, though I would have traded ten years of my life to have the talent to be part of her choreography for the *Flashdance* theme.

If there ever was a quintessential eighties jazz dance instructor, Bunni Thompson was it. Her long hair was sprayed and sculpted like a black flame. Sharp eye liner covered an underlying femininity and compassion. Two studded belts around her svelte waist completed the ensemble. Graciously, Bunni gave us all pink tees with black silkscreened lettering that read *Jazz Moves with the Bunni Thompson Dancers*. I would desperately endeavor to keep up with her choreography, to no avail.

I, among most of the others, would be relegated to a few simple steps at the end of the gala. The familiar synthesizer prelude to the theme song from *Fame* would be our signal to enter the ring for the finale. We all came out in the sections assigned. I managed to stay on the ring curb while doing a box step in time, sporting my oversized clown shoes. I spotted Mom and Dad beaming in the audience.

After the show, we students cleaned ourselves up. I looked sharp in my grey three-piece suit, the same one I wore for high school graduation five months ago. But in this strange type of graduation there was an underlying tension. The company provided us a sumptuous buffet, and the student clowns mingled with family who had come out to visit. Students and faculty greeted my parents; everyone had something nice to say. Perhaps the pure desperation of a boy in his teens appealed to them. It pleased me when Dad sarcastically said, "Too bad nobody likes you."

It pleased me to introduce Arnold Bramow, the Director of Special Projects, to my parents. He told them that I was a "hell of a guy." Arnold added that I did very well, and that he hoped I would be chosen. Mom would later remark on his expensive sweater.

After the festivities, we ended up giving my fellow student Karen a ride back to the Venice Villas. Dad drove, while Mom rode in the front seat of the rented sedan. Karen, a decade older, joked about "being in the backseat with Andy."

There was an after-party in one of the rooms at the Kent. Ivan, the artist hired to paint props, initiated a betting pool on how many of us would be chosen. It was a dollar to enter. There was a sense of resolve as we realized nothing more could be done. An air of giddiness entered the room. Guests and students were goofing around. A female ventriloquist was there as a visitor, using Mike, one of the two dwarves in the class, as her *dummy*.

I told myself I lived through something. Truly pursued it. This wasn't merely going through the motions, as I had conditioned myself to do from the ninth to the twelfth grade. This time I had given it my all. But was it enough?

I was in no hurry to walk across the grounds and go to bed. Frosty said we probably wouldn't sleep much the night before contracts were assigned. In my case, he was right.

In the morning, Frankie the dwarf burst into the room, along with Dana, a fellow student. But they came to wake up Brent, not me. Frankie yelled, "We made it!" I registered what was happening and managed to congratulate the trio. They left to joyfully sign their contracts, and I was left alone in the room. I wept as if a relative had died. I had to call Mom and Dad, who were staying at a nearby hotel.

Ann, forever considerate, had prepared a parting breakfast for the rest of us. I had no desire to eat. Visitors came as if for the viewing before a funeral. I would have died for Ringling. That morning, part of me did. Phil also got chosen, and his dad eventually came into my room. He asked me if I wanted a shot of whiskey. Ann came by also. She tried to comfort me. Ann said that I would have been a shoo-in if I had been four feet tall like Frankie and Mike. She sat with me and said, "Don't let them do this to you."

Mom and Dad made it over there eventually, and there was nothing much to say. I murmured, "I gave it everything." My mind flashed to Muhammad Ali, who said the same thing in an interview from the ring, moments after losing his title to Leon Spinks. Family gathered at one of the empty motel rooms, and I eventually joined them. The chosen ones were off at the arena signing their contracts and obviously celebrating. The other Kent Hotel students, with their next of kin, sat and made small talk. The day dragged. Packing could be done in a leisurely manner. The consistent heat in Florida can be soothing or an annoyance, depending on one's mood. Today it was the latter. Randy, one of the instructors, also came by to offer his condolences. Some of us milled about outside. We made awkward small talk. Randy joined our fidgeting, playing around with a cheap lawn chair. A disturbed lizard inside the aluminum tubing came to poke his head out. Randy inadvertently decapitated it by pressing down on the chair. The students had come there with a dream. For most of us the dream was broken that day. Some of our parents were there to commiserate with us. However, we were all somebody's children.

Rich, another rejected student, was downing Pixy Stix, those hideous paper tubes filled with sugar and chemical fruit flavoring. I absentmindedly accepted one that he offered. Rich had worked as a costume character of Pluto at Disney World.

Sometime in the hellish afternoon Don Arthur drove up to the Kent Hotel. He had been a magician by trade, and now served as the administrator at Clown College. I had returned to the funeral reception when I heard his familiar, friendly voice yell, "Andy Rose!" I murmured one or two obscenities and dashed outside. A few of us were hauled to the arena.

Irvin Feld was behind his desk. His son Kenneth was in the room, as well as Arnold Bramow. The younger Mr. Feld looked, no surprise, as if he'd been up all night choosing clowns for a circus. I now felt a hint of intimacy with *the company*, seeing him in an open-necked shirt. The son and dad were always natty in business suits for the public. Irvin still presented that image, sitting regally. Later, Mom and I would relate how he resembled Irving Rose, my grandfather. Seven of us would-be funsters were in the room. Kenneth proceeded, saying that we were chosen as alternates and told us to keep in touch. Irvin handed us his business card. There wasn't much to say, but I talked anyway. I tried to express eloquently my thought that the Greatest Show on Earth was more than a trademark. Kenneth said that was "nice," and then came the handshaking ritual. I reached across the desk to shake hands with Irvin and knocked over the cup of pencils on his desk. Arnold said that was a good clown gag. The room suddenly felt very small, and it was time to leave.

I got back to the hotel and entered through the sliding glass door, rejoining the bizarre reception. Then I announced that I had been chosen as an alternate. The initial shock had worn off. Those from the Kent Hotel who weren't chosen had seemingly accepted their fate. After all, they were older than I was and considerably more mature. Also, *his chosen clowns* from Kamp Kent had returned to the hotel, bringing positive energy. I stood on my knees and felt the comfort of the shag carpet beneath me. I think I was subconsciously saying a prayer of gratitude. I was also kneeling to talk at eye level with Frankie the dwarf. He advised me, in his heavy New York accent, to *"write to Mr. Felt every mont'."* The strange party eventually broke up and it was time to tie up loose ends. The bus from the Villas subsequently pulled in. Chris, a fellow student, who had obviously heard about my devastation earlier in the day, embraced me and chided, "You %&*#in' crybaby!"

The familiar grumble of the bus signaled once more that we were going to the arena. Upon arrival we milled about, congratulating those who earned it, consoling those who needed it. For both those who had won and lost, Clown College 1983 was history. Maybe I hadn't proven myself to be an outstanding clown, but perhaps more importantly, I survived a trying situation. I lived through something. I now sensed that Clown College seemed to bring out the best in me. Mr. Severini said that he hoped his son would turn out like me. I reached to shake his hand, and he pulled me in for a hug. A bigger person might say that this statement from the dean meant more than a contract. I wasn't a bigger person.

There was nothing to do but stroll through the quiet building for one last look. The facility was now tidy, and Clown College was tucked away. Not long thereafter, the Blue Unit would begin rehearsal for its world premiere. After Thanksgiving, they would rehearse, open the show, and hit the road in early 1984. Soon the arena would be bustling again. The only evidence of Clown College were the big grey garbage cans, which contained colorful remnants from the course. Discarded props of wood, fabric, and Styrofoam stuffed these containers. I wasn't sad when I saw in one of them a prop that I had used the night before. Time had been winding down a couple weeks prior, and I was desperate for a "walk-around." A walkaround is a brief sight gag used by clowns. Its practical function is providing entertainment during set-up for the following act.

Eventually, Rich and I joined forces on a cotton candy walk-around. Rich was the vendor, while I was the customer (sucker). A swatch of pink, fluffy fabric was wound around a conical Styrofoam swivel. Bilked, I walked away with the cotton candy stick, while Rich chuckled, holding the fabric. I chased him off. We presented the idea to Mr. Severini. He frowned silently, unimpressed but accepting the idea. The white cone and pink fabric now mocked me from the trashcan.

Mom and I would reflect upon the emotional state of her youngest child. There were things that she wouldn't tell me until later. How skinny I'd become. How Arnold Bramow and the others who ran Clown College, focusing on my *character*, were perhaps cueing me in to the fact that I hadn't quite made it into the first clown fleet. I know that if it was in Mom and Dad's power to get me a contract with Ringling, they would have enthusiastically done so. Dad would write a letter to Irvin Feld, expressing how impressed he was with the gala performance. He maintained what a memorable and valuable experience this was for me too, whether or not I would eventually be chosen as a clown.

After the parting pow wow at the arena, I regrouped with Mom and Dad. Since I was a small child, Mom, Dad, and I spent a great deal of time together, observing my older brother and sister at their various scholastic, athletic, and artistic functions. This practice evolved into *our* special time. Mom dubbed us *The Three Musketeers.* I think she was doing this to remind me that *I* was special too, despite the things my siblings did that always seemed more interesting. Now, it was my turn. For once I was coming into my own. The sun later set peacefully on the Three Musketeers in Florida's gulf coast. Dad had to fill the gas tank of the rental car. Mom and I giggled as we could hear him bragging about me to the attendant. I figured I hadn't given Dad reason to do much boasting until now. So much had happened since that June day of my high school graduation. My classmates who distinguished themselves with top marks got to wear white robes. Around twenty *popes,* easy to spot in the procession from the rest of us cardinals. This time I had truly reached for excellence. I had finished as an alternate, which was *something.*

Other than the Pixy Stick that Rich had given me, I hadn't eaten all day. It was time for my parents and me to share a victory meal of sorts. We found a Denny's. I joyfully downed chicken parmesan and spaghetti doused with generic, thick, red sauce, and a chocolate shake. We also experimented with *hush puppies,* fried balls of dough that are a staple in the South, new to us. The three of us sensed that a part of me had changed, if not my appetite. The next day Mom and Dad would have an earlier flight than me.

I had the opportunity to visit the Ringling Circus Museum in Sarasota, further anticipating the tradition that I was hoping to become a part of. I was awestricken to gaze upon a horse-pulled caravan that was long ago occupied by *The Wallendas,* a legendary high wire family. I found a souvenir program from the circus' 1956 season in the gift shop, on sale for $10. I proudly announced to the cashier that I was an alternate, chosen from the graduating Clown College Class, and she kindly gave me the magazine.

8. LIMBO

I got home and my parents sensed I needed to flop around the house a while. We were well into November, and the holiday season would be especially festive. Good old Al, a friend of the family who occasionally served as a handyman on projects in the house, dropped by during the ten AM hour. Mom had announced to him that I hadn't come back empty handed, chosen as an alternate. Al had served as a marine. He was little and loud. Since I'd met him as a boy, his classic method of displaying affection would be to hold me in a headlock. This time he hugged me.

The sheaves of Clown College were brought in, and now it was time to wait. Various ceremonies of the season came about. Al invited Dad and me to the awards banquet for the Modesto Junior College football team one more time. While Dad and Al fulfilled their duties as linesman to indicate first downs, I got to stand on the sidelines as a sidekick. Al embarrassed me at the banquet, announcing that I had run off to become a clown.

My brother and sister were away at college, and again it would be just Mom, Dad, and me. The Three Musketeers would ride again. In the chilly, foggy air of the Central Valley, Mom and I would delightfully hit the mall and McHenry Village for holiday preparations. There was still hope that I'd eventually get chosen by Ringling, but we gradually forged a *Plan B*. Because of Clown College, I had already missed what would have been my first term of higher education. At the mall we caught up with the president of Modesto Junior College, Dr. Lou Zellers, whose daughter Theresa was a friend of mine from high school. The always gregarious man seemed to take a shine to me. Naturally, he was encouraging when Mom and I informed him of the possibility that I would take a couple classes at MJC that spring to get my feet wet.

I would register for easy courses (*Film Appreciation* comes to mind), so I'd have a few credits under my belt if Ringling would never come a courtin'. Then I'd regroup at San Francisco State the following fall. I kept myself busy with errands, started driving an egg truck for Dad and cold calling as a salesman. For the most part, I was loafing. After what I'd gone through, Mom and Dad gladly let me have these weeks to goof off. Out of the blue I got a call from Aaron, a fellow graduate. He offered me the chance, with the other half dozen Clown College alumni from California, to appear in Barry Manilow's New Year's Eve concert.

The mood was lighthearted backstage at the Universal Studios Amphitheater as we applied our greasepaint. I had heard that Ringling owned the clowns' faces as registered trademarks. Overly cautious, I used a different make-up design. Our job was simple. In sharp contrast to Clown College, there was no pressure. We were instructed to wear red t-shirts that said *Barry Christmas* on them (yeah, I know) and hand out party favors to the audience coming in. At midnight we'd help Mr. Manilow pull a cord attached to a net, releasing balloons over the audience.

The wonders of Facebook have subsequently enabled some of us from Clown College to get reacquainted. Part of me yearns to return to that time when we were all fresh-faced kids in our teens and twenties. Maybe it's best to see everyone in my mind's eye, still that way. I think each of us were changed profoundly by the Clown College experience. In the final episode of the venerable TV show *M*A*S*H*, B.J. (Mike Farrell) talks to his best friend Hawkeye (Alan Alda) about getting together after the war. The men decide to leave their relationship in Korea. After all they went through, they reasoned, there would be no way to replicate what they had.

Nietzsche wrote, "Out of life's school of war—what doesn't kill me, makes me stronger." I believe I'm a better person after being run through the Clown College ringer. I hope the same is true for my fellow graduates.

I'll always remember Chris' and Spaghetti's kindness, taking me under their wings. The two were like big brothers. Chris turned up almost three decades later on Facebook. He had been working as a stilt walker at Margaritaville in Las Vegas. I eventually saw Spaghetti (whose reason for the nickname was a mystery) while on the road in Michigan. He was playing saxophone and tambourine, serving as sidekick to his brother Steve's band, the Dittlies. This fun-loving troupe tastefully sported thin ties and white dinner jackets, while doing a yeoman's job blasting covers from Rock and Roll's golden age. I loved all of those involved with Clown College '83.

On the TV show *Survivor,* the host, Jeff Probst, reads the names of those who got voted out of the competition. Sometimes there would be a remaining vote cast, but it wouldn't be relevant to the score. In such a case, the host proclaims that it would "remain a mystery." It was the same at Clown College. Those of us not chosen to go on the road never found out *why.* Twelve were initially offered contracts. Later, Frosty would confide in me that the Red Unit had cleaned house, getting rid of the *deadwood,* as he put it, and offering work to eleven graduates. The Blue Unit, largely a bastion of established journeyman clowns, gave work to only one Clown College student.

Six others, along with me, were chosen as alternates. For all I knew, I would be putting down the greasepaint forever. Anecdotes still trickle in online from those intensive weeks our class spent together. Kenny and Spaghetti had shared a room. Kenny said his Clown College roomie survived on beans. He reportedly left the pot on the stove and, at the end of the day, would simply scrape off the mold to have his dinner. Many years later when I talked to Spaghetti on the phone, he told me he'd be managing a restaurant in Detroit. I trust his culinary techniques had expanded some. We had always looked forward to *Atomic Bob*, Spaghetti's avant-garde theater pieces, which broke the tension during class gag presentations. Once, for whatever reason, Atomic Bob devoured an entire lemon in front of us, skin and all.

The surreal experience of Clown College was still with me as I waited and wondered. Two years later, my time with Ringling completed, I vacationed for a week in New York. I had the opportunity to see *Song and Dance,* with Bernadette Peters. In one number, *Tell Me on a Sunday,* she woefully awaited being informed of a relationship ending. I realized, as an alternate, that perhaps I'd never be told.

After the Barry Manilow concert, I was in no hurry to get home, and graciously freeloaded from relatives in Los Angeles. Uncle George and I were watching bowl games on Monday, January 2. The phone rang. Dad told me that Irvin Feld had called. Uncle George calmed me enough to avoid an infarction, and I phoned Ringling's corporate offices in Washington, D.C. I recall an episode of *The Dick Van Dyke Show,* in which Rob (Van Dyke) answers the phone and finds out the mayor is on the line. Van Dyke ridiculously combs his hair while talking to him. I was in a similar mindset. The senior Mr. Feld let me know that he had been talking to Kenneth, and they had decided, "Let's give Andy a chance." I suppose I managed to thank him and hang up. From the kitchen I heard Uncle George yawp from the living room. The wait was over.

After I left Ringling, Mom proclaimed that it came along too fast. According to her, it was a too much, too soon scenario, though now I wonder about that. I had spent the first eighteen years of my life vying to proclaim that I was special. Time and time again came the rejection, being compared to others who always seemed better than me. Now, as I hung up Uncle George's white push-button phone, my life would be validated, if only in my eighteen-year-old mind.

That holiday season would take me from Venice, Florida, to Uncle George's home in Venice, California. Soon I'd be back in Florida's Venice to begin rehearsals. I would fly home to Modesto the following day. My grandfather picked me up at Uncle George's house and drove me to the airport. As we waited for the plane, he advised me to be careful, especially in New York.

I'd have a few days to get ready. It was easy to throw together the items I needed. I hadn't really unpacked since coming home from Clown College. It seemed that for me Christmas came late that year, with the phone call from Mr. Feld.

Finally, I allowed myself to believe that this was true. My parents didn't belong to the Del Rio Country Club, down the street and across the railroad track from where we lived. At times, though, I'd sneak onto the golf course to be alone. The grass seemed to stretch forever on that brisk January night. I found myself somewhere in the middle of the links and screamed, "I'm Andy Rose, and I'm in the Greatest Show on Earth!"

9. FAMILIAR

Mom got busy making me an extra clown costume for the road. She used the shirt, pants, and vest patterns provided by my designer at Clown College. None of us in my family really had the chance to absorb the magnitude of what I was doing. The night before I left, it was only Mom, Dad, and me. Mom made a special dinner. I was packed and ready to go. Tomorrow the long journey to Florida would happen. Again. Mom and I cried. She brought up that this was a *trade-off.* I undoubtedly wanted to go on the road, but it meant months away from my family. We knew that things would be different after I had completed my adventure. She added that she and Dad couldn't have asked for a better son. That meant the world to me. This time I wouldn't be gone for just the summer. It would be almost a year.

I mused with my parents about the possibility that Ringling hired me as a good soldier as opposed to a good clown. Dad dismissed this notion, saying this was a perfect situation and that I should simply relax and enjoy it. In months to come I could have followed his advice more effectively.

I repeated the travel process, sitting for hours on a series of planes that took me from San Francisco to Venice, Florida. I remember the plastic listening device, resembling a stethoscope, that United Airlines assigned at the time. On screen was *Oxford Blues,* with Rob Lowe. A brash kid hustles his way into the renowned university, chasing his dream.

I finally arrived and walked into Clown Alley. This time, I was an employee. I bantered a bit with clowns from the Blue Unit, who were getting ready for a matinee. Soon they would be on the road with their new show, and it would be our turn to rehearse. There were some familiar faces. Richard, who had been dubbed *house mother* of the Kent Hotel, gestured that he couldn't shake my hand because he was applying his greasepaint. I also recognized Tommy, the boss clown. I auditioned for him, and it seemed a lifetime ago.

Kenneth Feld's two little girls scampered about Clown Alley, a special privilege for the owner's daughters. I pinched myself, still finding it hard to believe that I was actually *in* the Ringling Brothers and Barnum & Bailey Circus.

I made my way to the silver-colored train, my new home. The tracks were a half mile away from the arena. My space, one of a dozen closet-sized roomettes, was in the back of the car. Other *First of Mays* (first year clowns) from Clown College '83 greeted and congratulated each other. Veteran clowns welcomed us.

I would gradually piece together my living quarters. Between rehearsals I would forage for furnishings. I claimed an abandoned shelf outside of the train. With a few alterations from a handsaw borrowed from the Clown Alley toolbox, it tucked away nicely into the front left-hand corner. As a youngster I had proudly purchased a nine-inch black and white Sony TV for $135. It fit perfectly on the top shelf. Eventually, a failed walkaround idea became a second shelf. A vendor's box strapped to my chest, reading *Filet of Sole,* and me waving the sole of a shoe to the audience. No, the owners of the show didn't think it was funny either, so I ended up nailing the box to the wall of my roomette. Wooden boxes on either end of the floor were known as *gauchos,* providing more storage space. In one of them I tucked away my money in a coffee can. A piece of plywood connected the gauchos. Cushions were placed on top, and that was my bed. A fellow clown had a half-full quart of yellow paint, so I gave him a dollar in exchange for it. He courteously threw in a Beck's beer. A few old circus posters (I was literally eating, drinking, *and* sleeping circus) completed my interior decoration.

I was eager to contribute to the show in any way possible. I volunteered to ride a contraption three wheels high. But unlike a six-foot unicycle, I couldn't *idle* on it, pedal slightly back and forth to stay in one place. There was only one way to go, forward. I practiced pedaling around the hippodrome track and caught on, little by little. I joyfully waved at Irvin Feld in his office as I practiced and was thrilled when he smiled and waved back. It was the same office where I first met Mr. Feld and then was deemed an alternate after Clown College.

Because I was an alternate, I hadn't signed my contract when rehearsals had begun. I started pestering Wayne, the boss clown, who assured me there was no problem. Stupidly, I had set the stage for annoying my supervisor, which would become the basis of our relationship.

Finally, I was sent to see Tim Holst, the performance director. A small room above the seats at the far end of the arena served as his office. We both sat down, and my new boss could tell I was nervous. He acknowledged that I wasn't sporting my customary grin and that I had a great smile. Mr. Holst presented me with a stack of typed papers, and there was an awkward silence. Part of me wanted to take my time and peruse the contract at leisure. However, my boss was waiting, and I didn't want to test his patience. I would be doing that plenty in the months ahead. I took a cursory look at the document and signed my name. A couple months ago, I was wearing a circular number thirty-five on my chest, parading my wares among other Ringling hopefuls. The gala performance had occurred at this end of the arena, where we performed for the audience in the seats below Mr. Holst's office. At the time I didn't know this room existed. With my signature on the line, I was now officially a member of the Greatest Show on Earth. At the same time, I was still an awkward teenager, over-whelmed by my surroundings.

My new duties, including the arena choreography, intimidated me at first, but I gradually caught on. I was forging for myself a new way of life. Over time there would be a routine. Little by little I adapted, through trial and error. Issues came up during rehearsals, but nothing devastating. Another new hire, a blonde showgirl, and I appeared to hit it off. Sadly, she was abruptly dropped from the show, for reasons that were never made clear. One night I bor-rowed another clown's folding bicycle, which fit in an overhead storage area on the train. I was riding it when a car mirror sideswiped my elbow, hit and run. I needed stitches and was obviously lucky that it wasn't worse. I didn't bother telling my parents, not wanting to worry them. I subsequently received an urgent message to call home. My consideration had the opposite effect; the ambulance bill had been mailed to my parents' house.

I didn't always use my head, but I always had passion. I was now living the Ringling dream. What better way to symbolize that the show was *in my blood,* than to give blood? In retrospect, I could have held off on that one. I had enough on my plate as a rookie clown. The Ringling organization had a blood drive for Don Foote, the costume designer. Sadly, he wouldn't survive his terminal illness. I didn't know Mr. Foote but felt a tremendous sense of loyalty now that I was part of the company. I gave blood for the first time, which happened to be the day of our first run through of the show. I figured it was the right thing to do and was reassured when Tim Holst entered the bloodmobile and acknowledged that I was donating.

Afterward, there was just enough time to put on my makeup before getting out on the floor. I grabbed a piece of pie from the employees' cafeteria, thinking it would be a good idea to keep my blood sugar up. Behind the curtain, while we were getting ready to go on, Frosty was there to help get our season rolling. He could see that I was nervous. Frosty calmed me some, mentioning that this was quite an experience for a kid my age. While we were on the floor during *come-in* (when clowns warm up the audience), I nearly passed out while wheeling a prop from the floor but made it through the rest of the performance without any problems.

A show would have a run of two seasons. I joined the Red Unit on its second year of the tour. This was known as the rodeo route. The rehearsal period was brief, and opening night soon rolled around. I made sure to put on my greasepaint early. Then I took some time to sit alone in the arena before *doors* was called. The bright blue seats and drab green rubber on the hippodrome track were familiar. In front of the red and white backdrop, in yellow letters on a crimson background, was spelled out *RINGLING BROTHERS AND BARNUM & BAILEY CIRCUS*. Above was hung the familiar globe logo, with *THE GREATEST SHOW ON EARTH,* in bold white caps. At last, it happened. Ringling had become my place of employment. I truly appreciated it and didn't take it for granted.

I sported my greasepaint and the standard t-shirt and gym shorts. This was my Clown College attire. Now, however, I was a clown by profession. I belonged there. Then again, maybe not yet, as I would later find out as a first-year clown. Still, this moment, it was perfect. George Burns sang a song called *I Wish I Was 18 Again.* I sat and gazed down on the arena floor as the time for my first performance as a Ringling clown approached. I wouldn't mind living that moment once more. Then I think further about my eighteenth year and shudder at what I survived.

That same arena seemed to taunt me as I had slogged through Clown College. It's safe to say that no student in the history of the school wanted a contract with the show more than I did. Now, instead of Clown College paraphernalia on the floor, an efficiently elaborate set of rigging was on display. Cables, ropes, and lights, precisely placed, indicated that this was it, *the show.* Those of us in greasepaint would no longer be merely training and wishing. Now we'd be performing in specially designed costumes, categorized for our own respective places on the floor. At eighteen, it was almost too much to absorb. Was I Icarus, flying too close to the Ringling sun on wings of wax?

My only clear memory of the first performance of the season was a sense of terror during the opening number. Suddenly, the choreography dictated that I, in a chorus of a half dozen clowns, be on the front of the hippodrome track. The audience, I panicked, would be watching *me.* Gratefully, as far as I know, no snapshots exist which capture that moment. My expression must have been something other than a clown's wide smile. Crandall Diehl, one of the choreographers, mouthed the words *calm down.* He looked at me as if I were about to drop a Ming vase. Regan, who was one of the showgirls, became my dance partner and nemesis. She had messed with my mind by warning me of a previous clown and man child like me who was fired for his immaturity. During the rehearsal period, I lived in fear that I would meet the same fate.

Before we knew it, the show was wrapped up in Venice, and we were on the road to Orlando. Usually, one town ran uneventfully into the next on the rodeo route, and we played smaller cities. Orlando was an exception. In one of Gunther Gebel-Williams' appearances, he and a tiger perched on horseback made their way around the hippodrome track. But this time the skittish cat jumped off and started running around in the audience! The entire cast was on the floor, and all we could do was continue our choreography as Mr. Williams jumped into the audience to retrieve his cat.

My problems on the road were never due to laziness or malice. In my foolish youth, I figured the recipe for success in the circus was working hard and treating people well. But I neglected to see that a key factor was also taking my head out of the sand and paying attention to what was going on around me. Stilt walkers were irritated with me once or twice when I momentarily got in their way during the opening production number. Like any teenager, there were times when it seemed as if I couldn't do anything right. I called home crying. "I'm just a boy," I wailed. Mom replied that unfortunately, I had a man's job. She asked me if I wanted to come home. "I can't," I declared.

Under another boss, the decision to pack up my bags and leave the show would have been made for me. But Tim Holst, the performance director, wasn't another boss and showed infinite patience. Mr. Holst consistently had a knowing look in his eye, as he bailed me out of one screw-up after another. After meeting Mr. Holst, Mom related to me his concern that I was being teased by the other clowns. She recalled Mr. Holst asking if the teasing bothered me. My response was, "It's been happening my whole life." Mr. Holst recognized that after months on the road, I was still an overwhelmed teenager. Graciously, he cut me considerable slack. Once I told him that other clowns were purposefully bumping into me during a production number. His simple response was the Theodore Roosevelt quote, "Speak softly, and carry a big stick." The next performance, during that number, he looked at me from behind the curtain, a baseball bat in his hand.

Others in Clown Alley complained that I was too young to be there, and maybe I was. I'm grateful that a few hurt feelings along the way was all the price I paid, considering. My boss clown at Carson & Barnes had related to me a story about a brash young clown being beaten beyond recognition by some elephant handlers. There was also a story about a gifted trapeze flyer getting on the wrong side of jealous competitors. Rumor has it they broke both of his arms. I didn't want it to be so, but I found out that the circus world could be a cruel one.

There were many instances during my first season when it would have been easier to go home. However, that was never really an option. Over time I discovered that I was beginning to win the respect of those around me. As months passed, concessionaires, showgirls, musicians, and some of the other clowns recognized my level of character. And there were moments of interspersed splendor that made the whole experience seem worthwhile. We had the Fourth of July off in Alabama. Several of us from the show piled into a cab and paid the driver some fifty dollars to take us to the beach. We ended up in Fairhope and flopped for the day on the sand. It was rare to have a day on the beach with friends and fried chicken. As much as I adored life on the road, I treasured instances of being a normal person on a normal day off. We stayed into the night. I stood alone in warm water up to my chest, watching fireworks fill the sky and reflecting in an exquisite blackness on Mobile Bay. I hadn't been there before, or anywhere close by. Still, at that moment, I never felt more at home.

10. KNOCKS

The Clown College application had been a strange document. It asked numerous personal questions, such as "When was the last time you cried?" and "If you could be anybody else, whom would you choose?"

Also, we were instructed to provide a response to the cliché, familiarity breeds contempt. Perhaps I should have given more consideration to the reason Ringling management used this saying. I surmise they were trying to get a read on our reaction to being around a group of people twenty-four hours a day. If there was someone I liked, the best of friendships could become strained through this proximity. If there was someone I didn't like, it was impossible to ignore him. It was a type of marriage, one in which we were together behind the curtain, on the arena floor, and at home on the train. In the Broadway play *A Chorus Line,* Zach, the director, explains that he's choosing eight people who can work together. He isn't merely searching for good dancers. I believe that the officials of Clown College used a similar methodology. We were subject to long hours working together. What's more, a dozen apprentice clowns would share a train car. While we had our own small space to sleep, any cooking or other personal needs would be done communally.

I don't take my time alone for granted, the opportunity to simply *be.* On the road, literally any time I left my 3'x6' cubicle, I was forced to present myself in a particular way. Over time, I discovered that the arenas we played provided sanctuary. I'd hop on the 8:30 AM bus, hours before the other clowns would arrive, and have the place to myself. In a sense I was a marionette, placed back into my little box to rest at night.

Life always seemed to be a process of moving to the next thing, and it was no different in the circus. Carson & Barnes became a vehicle for Clown College. Clown College became a vehicle for Ringling. Rehearsals began, and we were often in the arena morning, noon, and into the evening. We'd report at 10 AM and stand in line as Mr. Holst inspected daily the ranks of Clown Alley. We collaborated with wardrobe and prop specialists, while waiting to be called to the floor for production numbers with the choreographers. In the early evening, we'd have a dinner break, and then would come back to practice our gags. The hours were not wearing, so much as the recognition that I didn't really know what I was doing. As a *First of May*, a circus rookie, I would find my job was basically to shut up, do what I was told, and stay out of the way. Kind old Lou Jacobs, who had been at this game for six decades, comforted me by saying that it got easier once we were on the road.

To a degree he was right. The show remained the same. Once I knew the timing of the routines and my two left feet mastered the choreography of the production numbers, the performance became a cakewalk. Instead of sitting back and enjoying the ride, I looked for new challenges. For a while, I assisted another clown and the head electrician with set-up and tear down, configuring the lights on the arena floor. I earned $35 for each plugging and unplugging. It took the better part of a day to unload the lighting equipment and make the appropriate connections. After the final performance, we'd pull the cables and pack the lights up in boxes in their proper places on a truck. I was no better suited to this type of work than I was for setting up and taking down the trapeze rigging at Carson & Barnes. That *cherry pie* job didn't last long.

On a call home to Mom and Dad, I announced that I had started to become a proficient juggler. I decided to quit my extra work setting up the lights and focus on my juggling between shows. I imagined becoming adept to the point where I would have my own act in Las Vegas, but after my second year on the road, this ambition gave way to the more practical pursuit of a college degree.

Sometimes my mind wanders back to that frighteningly enthralling first season with Ringling, wishing I could change it. It's a bit like seeing myself as Ebenezer Scrooge, guided on a video tour of his life by *The Ghost of Christmas Past.* Scrooge let go of the woman he loved decades ago, screaming at the image of himself for being the fool he was. However, as Scrooge found in the end, one can learn from the past and then let it go. Some, like myself, were still at a very young and impressionable age. I understand the importance of forgiveness. Forgiving myself and them. We experienced something extraordinary on the road together. I believe that this is what should be celebrated. All bitterness should be gone forever, like a pebble dropped from the vestibule of a train car, as we roll into the next town.

11.   CONTRACT

St. Louis was our stop on the tour where contracts for the next season would be determined. I was the youngest clown in the alley, disliked by many. At home a helpful member of my clan would be there to bail me out of yet another screw-up. By now I had learned the hard truth. The circus world wouldn't take care of me like family.

The pipeline from Clown College to the traveling show always provided the possibility of new faces. There were twenty-six of us, and all of us knew we were replaceable. The exception was the legendary Lou Jacobs, our professor emeritus.

It also seemed so for Duane Thorpe, who managed to hang around Clown Alley for thirty-six years. Even old Duane would be ousted at the end of the 1986 season. Duane, who went by *Uncle Soapy*, selected some Clown Alley denizens to pal around with on train runs, and I was never one of them. However, occasionally he'd throw a nice remark my way, like when he said Irvin Feld liked me. In addition, occasionally he would talk to me about years past with Ringling, because I was an avid listener. I was fascinated when he described how police detectives interviewed the clowns in 1965 at Madison Square Garden. On April 21 of that year, the body of clown Paul Jung was found murdered in a midtown Manhattan hotel. With contracts coming up, I confided in Duane how much I wanted to come back the following season. Born some forty years before me, he starkly imparted the sage wisdom that you don't always get what you want.

Each clown would be called in to talk with Kenneth Feld, who took over after his father died of a stroke. The torch was passed, and the show would go on. We killed time as the day melted. Good soldiers, ready at any time to meet for our briefing. We would either be asked to return or allowed to stick around until the season ended in Cleveland. One by one, we were called in. Frankie the dwarf had been my buddy at Clown College, despite my hitting him with a prop on the chin. He ended up being my next-door neighbor on the train. At times he was still kind to me, but frequently had a way of kicking me when I was down. This would be one of those times. Half a dozen nervous clowns sat around the corner of the arena set up for the band. Clown Alley at this point seemed claustrophobic. The inevitable subject came up. Frankie bitterly announced his hope that I wouldn't be invited back.

Contract day was a well-oiled part of the Ringling machine. Those asked to return would sign their contracts. It would be an exit interview of sorts for the clowns who wouldn't be returning, either by their own choice or that of management.

Eventually I was called into the next phase of the waiting process. Performance director Tim Holst seemed to have sympathy for a teenager with more heart and desire than common sense. Mr. Holst had set out a ball with jacks in his temporary office, something to occupy the clowns in waiting. Sometime before, while we were getting ready to go out on the floor, he touched the lapel of my sequined production blazer and asked if I wanted to return the following year. The suit was in the set of costumes I had admired as a spectator in Oakland while waiting to become a Clown College student. I expressed my desire to return and asked if he wanted me to come back. "Sure, *I* do," was his reply. Another link up the chain of command approved of me. That gave me hope.

I broke the ice with Mr. Holst by saying that it was a rough year for everybody. I was referring to the numerous times he took my side during squabbles in Clown Alley, but also alluding to the recent tragedies the show had experienced. In addition to the passing of Irvin Feld, our chimpanzee trainer Mickey Antalek had died of a heart attack. My nervousness subsided a bit when Mr. Holst proclaimed, "Next year will be a better one, won't it?" To me this implied my inclusion in *next year,* and I perked up.

Finally, I got called in. Allen Bloom, a longtime right hand for the Feld organization, was in the room, and I introduced myself.

Bloom had been with Irvin Feld since he managed Paul Anka as a teen heartthrob. There was a pizza box on a table, but I wisely didn't ask for a slice. Kenneth Feld told me to sit down. He had a heart and could see how much Ringling meant to me. Mr. Feld also knew how young and impressionable I was and decided to use the *scared straight* technique. The fact that I was being picked on by several of my fellow clowns was no secret. He indicated that the easiest thing to do under these circumstances would be to let me go. Then he said that I was a "pretty good clown out there," and would have to rise above those who were picking on me. I wisely kept my mouth shut when he added that I had to get my head screwed on straight for the following season. I left with a contract in my hand. I walked into Clown Alley and was congratulated by those who were hanging out by their trunks.

Some of us signed the contract for the next season. Others chose not to return. A few weren't invited on the road for the following year. As the individualized meetings carried over into the afternoon, the resulting changes in personnel naturally brought a damper to the morale in Clown Alley. One by one, more returned. He would either be holding the stapled white papers or not. It was easy to empathize with those who weren't chosen to return the following season. I knew that it could easily have been me.

Plans for acts in the upcoming version of the show were also arranged. A substantial number of the animal trainers and acrobats would be moving on, too. I was saddened when my buddy Irvin Hall, the baboon trainer, told me behind the curtain that he wouldn't be coming back the following year. Nevertheless, he expressed happiness for me when I said that I would be returning. A large portion of the performers' personal interactions occurred when we were lined up, getting ready for one of our production numbers. The space behind the curtain was our *water cooler* of sorts. Whatever we were experiencing behind the scenes, the job required us to be smiling and waving to the crowd once the red and white striped curtain opened. Then, behind the curtain again, we would get back to our lives. Naturally, there were a lot of these powwows as the remainder of the season wound down. For those who were asked back, it was a time of elation. Still, we knew we had to curb our enthusiasm in respect for those who wouldn't be returning.

That night I had a date and was in a hurry to shower and be on my way. I wrapped myself in a towel, greasepaint still on. Leaping across Clown Alley to the showers, I barely missed knocking over Kenneth Feld, who happened to be walking down the corridor.

My date and I drove somewhere for dinner. Behind us, a half mile away, a huge silver-colored half oval, the Saint Louis Arch, seemed to greet me warmly.

12. ROUTINE

In a typical week we would work six days. Often Monday would be off, and that was when we'd roll on to the next stop. We usually did two shows a day and three on Saturdays. Every few weeks a new route card came out, telling us the name of upcoming cities and dates. On the rodeo route it usually didn't matter where we were playing. One small city was indistinguishable from another, and we would be there only three to four days at a time. Our job stayed the same; the geographic location didn't matter. Occasionally an amusing diversion would come up, like when I could legally belly up to a bar at eighteen in Topeka, Kansas.

And then there was Boston, one of a smattering of big cities we played that season. The show featured several clowns jumping from a mini trampoline, doing forward flips over elephants. The finale of the act featured an acrobat jumping over four of them. The timing was perfect when my friend and fellow clown Rick replaced the acrobat. We were in his hometown, and he had friends and family taking up an entire section of the Boston Garden. Rick fearlessly cleared the "four ponderous pachyderms," as Dinny the ringmaster announced. Behind the curtain we mobbed him as though he'd hit a game winning homer in the World Series. An event like that, on the home stretch of a long season, was truly welcome in Clown Alley.

While it was easy to portray joy on the floor when things went well, a hard part of the job was hiding sadness on cue. In Memphis I visited Graceland, Elvis' celebrated mansion. The cab arrived at the arena just in time to put on my greasepaint and costume for the performance. I placed the letter from my friend Theresa in my trunk. Between numbers I read that a mutual friend, Katrina, died in a car accident. As always, the job required me to block out whatever was happening as a human being and return to the audience with a smile.

The familiar lament was that we were working too hard. This was heard most often before the Saturday 11 AM performance. A clown would whine about the ease of life back home. Sleeping in and watching *Soul Train*. Another would exasperatingly blurt out, "Who's the %+@*ing %#*@ who wrote this schedule?" I remained quiet when this subject came up; there was nowhere in the world that I'd rather be.

By move-out night I'd be contentedly weary to the bone. Scrubbed clean of my greasepaint, with time to decompress, my trunk would be packed for the next town. We usually wouldn't stray far from the train; there was no precise time of departure. One night in Charleston, South Carolina, a local lady took several of us out on the town. We lost track of time and feared the train would move on without us. After setting new speed records in her station wagon, she talked a cop out of giving her a ticket. We made it safe and sound back to the clown car. Eventually, she married a member of the Blue Unit's Clown Alley and became a clown for the show herself.

I'd often be sound asleep by the time the train would start moving. It took a while to connect the cars. If I awakened, the rhythmic rolling of the wheels on tracks would rock me tenderly back to slumber.

At some point, I'd stir back into consciousness; it didn't matter when. I'd look out my window and see the earth moving by; it was impossible to keep from smiling. Time stood still in my little self-contained world. The location of my roomette, in the back end of the car, made it easy for me to slip out to the vestibule. The tiny porch between cars provided fresh air and an occasional wave from a local as we would pass. In his song, *Turn the Page,* Bob Seger tells of the tedium of riding sixteen hours on a tour bus. I never saw the train runs as stifling or confining. This was found time. A chance to read or write a letter home. If I wanted to venture out, the *pie car* was a few cars down. Cheap, passable diner food was served to order, but it was also a gathering place. There were a few tables, and the décor consisted of old prints of painted clown faces.

I might stop on the way and visit with someone. Train runs were leisurely, no need to hurry. Occasionally, I'd be invited into someone's *state room* for a chat. Such coveted living space was assigned to those further up in the organization's pecking order. A state room was about three times the size of a roomette; a small group could gather in one of them.

Long trips on the rodeo route through the Midwest and South became routine. I welcomed the adventure. The June and July I spent with Carson & Barnes had planted seeds of wanderlust. In many ways my mudshow experience helped me appreciate Ringling more. This was a comparatively plush means of travel. Train runs also afforded me some time to myself, a scarce commodity in Clown Alley.

I lived in California for the first seventeen years of my life. We never came close to my home state on the rodeo route. Life was now full of adventure, far away from Modesto. There were times when the train would abruptly stop, and we'd hop out and walk around a while. Somewhere in the South I found myself strolling along the rails on a sunny afternoon. Dry, pale-yellow grass swished gently beneath my sneakers. Girls' voices in the distance grew louder as they approached. Two black girls appeared, about twelve years old. I froze, bewildered. Now, about twenty yards away, I realized they were shouting at me. Evidently, they were marking their territory, and I wasn't welcome. They rushed toward me, yelling and throwing little scraps of garbage they grabbed from the ground. I was lucky that they couldn't find any rocks or bottles at their feet. At first, merely perplexed, I then registered what was happening. I started to get scared. I looked to my left at the line of silver train cars for sanctuary, about thirty yards away. Then my eighteen-year-old pride kicked in, and I felt embarrassed and ashamed for fearing a couple of little girls.

A black concessions guy that I'd seen in passing on bus rides to the arena came to my rescue. He was also walking around and saw what was happening. A loud *"Hey!"* did the trick, and the girls stopped what they were doing. I thought it wise to get back to my car immediately. When I had time to think about what had happened, I was filled with sadness. What had caused these girls to automatically hate me? I wanted to ask them and find out but knew I couldn't.

Usually, it was uneventful as the train rolled to a stop in a remote yard. Occasionally there would be something noteworthy to see. In Boston the train parked behind MIT. In Dallas it was stationed behind the Cotton Bowl.

In the evening, I'd settle in the roomette and gradually transition myself back into clown mode. Perhaps a local TV station would be playing a classic movie. I was raised on evening television, but now it was only an occasional treat because of the show schedule. Monday Nights, usually off, gave me the chance to watch *Call to Glory,* with Craig T. Nelson. The heroic Colonel Raynor Sarnac, a rugged individualist Navy pilot, would see me through the beginning of another week.

On move-in day the clowns would report to the arena on the 2:30 PM bus. Before leaving the train, I'd catch an episode of *As the World Turns,* which my mom and sister followed. Meg Ryan, sprightly and flirtatious in her youth as Betsy, would have made a good clown. Then it was time to go back to work. I appreciated the solitude in my roomette but was always ready to return to the arena. I felt a little like a thoroughbred by this time, skittish and eager to run again.

Apprentice clowns, those in their first three years, were required to show up for *trunks,* unloading our performance equipment and setting up at the building. It was mostly standing around. With that task completed, we were free to do what we wanted until it was time to put on our greasepaint and get ready for the show.

With each new city there was a faint sense of being lost. I wasn't on the road long enough to return to these locations a second time. There was always a newness both enticing and disorienting. I'd have my greasepaint on early and would mill about the arena before Opening Night. Eventually "Doors!" was bellowed out, and the audience would start filing in. For a few more days in this town, be it Des Moines, Peoria, or Kalamazoo, I'd make the transition from teenager to clown. Ringmaster Dinny McGuire's familiar baritone would resonate, "Ladies and gentlemen, the world-famous Ringling Brothers and Barnum & Bailey clowns." It was time for *come-in,* when we would warm up the audience. I had brought a cornet that I started playing in the fifth grade, so I had a spot in the clown band. The first year we marched out in sombreros and played the *Mexican Hat Dance.* A clown would hit a prop with a metal box that was made to look like a piñata. Frankie the dwarf would pop out with pistols, shooting at us as we ran out. The show was underway.

In the *Aerobics* gag, another clown and I were in drag, sporting outlandish warm up suits with padded bras. We wore inflated rubber balls attached to springs underneath our pants, giving the illusion of bulbous behinds. The fake breasts and butts made us look like overweight women in an aerobics class. Colleen the clown, rail thin, played *straight woman* in the bit, the lady aerobics instructor determined to work us into shape. She put us through a battery of calisthenics until, exasperated, we decided we had had enough. My portly partner and I would then push Colleen into the "steam box," and a puff of smoke would come out. Mike the dwarf, dressed in an identical orange warm-up suit as Colleen, would jump out of the box and chase us off. The smoke was created by a *squib,* which we learned to make in Clown College. Gunpowder was packed tightly into a piece of a plastic garbage bag, then wire was wrapped around it. The gunpowder would be detonated when touched with another piece of metal. One night Mike thought it would be hilarious to squib my roomette. I came close to having an infarction when a billowy cloud awoke me with a bang.

Opening marked the official beginning of the show. Clowns often complained about the heavy weight of the production costumes worn during arena choreography four times in each performance. The jackets and pants included substantial lining so they would last for two years. Back at Carson & Barnes, the boss clown expressed his disdain for these production numbers, proclaiming that the clowns were being used as chorus boys.

My t-shirt would be soaked with sweat by the time *finale* came. I had three different sets of embellished clothes for the production numbers. In *opening* and *finale,* we wore the same costumes. *Spec,* which gave way to intermission and *menage,* near the end of the show, each had its own outfit. In circus vernacular, it was pronounced *manage.* That was when Gunther Gebel-Williams would put the elephants through their paces.

I was one of the clowns who wore a *bubble suit,* a one-piece affair so named because of the puffy sleeves and legs. The entire number was color-coordinated in black, silver, and yellow. I happened to be the last clown off the floor and was assigned an additional duty. Mr. Williams would at times perform the amazing feat of being flipped in the air from a teeterboard by an elephant. I would spot whether the teeterboard was in place, as we ran backstage to Clown Alley. My announcement of "teeterboard" meant that we'd have a few extra minutes to prepare for finale. If I yelled, "no teeterboard," we had to dress for the final number immediately. Even if I had a few extra minutes, I would be there early if the teeterboard was set up, never tiring of what would take place before my eyes.

I have never seen a more amazing interaction of man and beast than the elephant teeterboard display. An elephant would trot with a running start. She had the delicacy to push a front foot down on one end of a seesaw, and Mr. Williams would be standing on the other end. He would be propelled into the air, then land standing on the back of another elephant. As if this wasn't enough, Mr. Williams then had the elephant perform the maneuver again. This time he would do a back flip and execute a perfect three-point landing.

The night's performance over, I'd shower, and usually catch the second bus back to the train. I'd often catch the 8:30 bus the next morning. I've never been much of a night owl. Sometimes I'd watch David Letterman for a while before falling asleep. I had an alarm clock but didn't need it. On Friday nights I would turn in as early as possible. Saturday would be long, with three performances. I'd think about waking up the next morning and being in greasepaint in time for the 10:40 come-in, before the 11 AM show. I grew accustomed to letting NBC's *Friday Night Videos* lull me to sleep. This mainstay of the eighties became a fond companion. Wang Chung, Huey Lewis, and Cyndi Lauper serenaded me to sleep. The following day I'd be in greasepaint for twelve hours.

Saturdays would move slowly, and we were worn out by the time the evening's show rolled around. Father Jack Toner, our chaplain, would officiate Mass inside of Ring Two between the second and third performances. I often attended services, watching my friend work. Sundays seemed to pass quickly. Usually there was a show in the early evening, and we were back home around nightfall. This was often when the show would pack up and leave. I loved this time. After arriving back at the train, there was a sense of calm stillness in my roomette. As the evening wore on, I felt the familiar series of thumps as the rail cars connected to travel through the night.

Despite the repetition, I was never bored. I knew that I was out there to shine, and so I did. I wasn't even bothered too much by having to dance with Regan, my overbearing Amazon dance partner. As a skinny, awkward eighteen-year-old, I was no match for the six-foot tall, muscular drill sergeant. I dutifully learned the steps of our forty-five seconds of shared choreography and managed to stay off of her feet. I didn't mind letting her lead. My mother knew that Regan and I couldn't stand each other and delighted in watching us work together. Mom contended that although we moved our feet perfectly in unison, we refused to make eye contact. She made a reference to Richard Burton and Elizabeth Taylor, who were forced to work together after their divorce. Over time, Regan and I laughed about our ongoing feud. Backstage, getting ready to go on for the finale, we'd sarcastically refer to ourselves as *Fred and Ginger*.

The acrobats and animal trainers, most of them in circus families, were usually little more than nodding acquaintances. However, Irvin Hall, the eternally jolly baboon trainer, became a close friend. The two of us forged a camaraderie as I'd come into the arena early. He invited me a couple times to travel with him to the next town. Our backgrounds were completely different, but we had a common love of the circus. Life on the road was all he knew, coming from a circus family of ten generations. He had appeared in *Ripley's Believe it or Not* as a two-year-old, the youngest boy to ever ride a unicycle. Irvin and his siblings also appeared on the *Ed Sullivan Show,* riding their unicycles as *Mel Hall's Whiz Kids.* For Irvin, going to college and getting a "real" job would have been every bit as foreign to him as my joining the circus was to me.

On one run between cities, we visited the *Bentley Brothers Circus* in Kansas City, where Irvin had family members presenting a bear act. Another time we caught the Iowa State Fair. We also stopped in Baraboo, Wisconsin, to see the Circus World Museum. I noticed a real sense of fellowship by these circus lifers. They also seemed to appreciate that I was interested in their craft. Irvin travelled in a small truck that looked like one of my dad's egg delivery vehicles. Only this truck hauled baboons, not eggs. Once at a truck stop, sometime in the middle of the night, I heard a blood-curdling scream. There's nothing like being awakened at three AM by quarrelling baboons.

Naturally, it was special when my parents came to the show. My role as an apprentice clown was largely a supporting one. Finding me in the three rings of controlled chaos took some effort.

After three months of my being on the road, Mom needed to visit her youngest child. The rodeo route wouldn't be coming through California, so they'd have to get on a plane to see me. My mother, father, and sister coordinated their schedules to visit while we were playing Knoxville, Tennessee. During the bicycle display, the clowns rode across the hippodrome track to the sound of *Daisy, Daisy*. We mugged to the audience while riding various types of motorless vehicles. One clown hunkered down over a tiny tricycle. Others rode in a tandem. Another merry maker perched atop a retro bike that had a giant wheel with the pedals attached directly to it. I perched on a contraption with three wheels, one stacked atop the other. I pedaled from the top wheel, and the machinery moved forward. It was the one appearance in the show where I was easy to spot. I saw my father waving from the audience and yelled, "Dad!" The last time my parents had seen me perform was at the Clown College gala performance a few months before. Now I was actually in the show.

My schedule allowed us to spend mornings together, and in the afternoon, they would drop me off at the arena to get ready. Like any teenage boy, I fretted that my mother would embarrass me. As my parents pulled up in the car, we saw a bare-chested Gunther Gebel-Williams hosing down his RV. Full of horror, I turned to my mother and beckoned to her, "Don't look!" I was fearful that she would act like a crazed fan. Later, Dad wisecracked to Mom, "You have no idea how close you came to being turned into a pillar of salt."

My family visited once more that season when we played Houston in July. This was a more laid-back experience, because on weekdays we only had an evening performance. The hotel where my family stayed adjoined *The Summit,* the arena where we played. This time, in addition to my brother and sister, my paternal grandparents came along. We gathered to commemorate my parents' twenty-fifth anniversary.

The trade-off of having such a close-knit family was the months spent away from them. My correspondence and phone calls were often somber. I forced myself to *turn on the light switch* during performances and literally felt my jaws get sore from forced smiling. Behind the curtain I sensed that my colleagues weren't really interested in discussing my chronic homesickness. I called collect and ran up my parents' phone bills to ridiculous levels. I maintained how much I loved performing in the show, despite being away from home. Mom cheerfully noted that the high I achieved in front of audiences wasn't "illegal, immoral, or fattening." I also recall a letter from my sister Lynne, reminding me to enjoy myself. She added, "You're in the circus, for chrissakes!"

13. FRIEND

The train pulled into Providence, Rhode Island, on a sunny afternoon. I figured that this would be like any other town on the rodeo route. Life on the road was in full swing as I puttered about my tiny space on the train. Stolen moments like these, for chores around my roomette, were quite welcome. We'd already been on the road for months, but I was still trying to get my living space just so. Like anybody, I always had something to do around the house. On this day, I was scraping glue from my walls, left behind by unsightly carpet squares I had discarded. Two young ladies approached the train, looking around curiously. I stepped into the vestibule, and we began to chat. One of them, Sue, would become my friend for life.

Sue was short, had brown curly hair, and an infectious smile. She would have made a good clown herself. Sue would later come to visit the show, bringing friends and family with her. We'd write letters back and forth while I was on the road. It was Sue who mainly held up the friendship, however. As a typical teenage boy, I was prone to irresponsibility. Once I had completely forgotten a lunch date I had with her and her mom and sister, but my good-natured buddy always forgave me.

At the time she attended Johnson and Wales College. There I was exposed to the fun side of higher education, outside of classes and studying. I wondered how these kids got any work done, downing so many melon balls and sloe gin fizzes. This experience reinforced my own desire to become a college student when I was ready. Sue also played a role in my decision to leave the circus and go to college. When the topic of higher education came about, she always nudged me in that direction.

I enjoyed being around young people with East Coast sensibilities. Despite their partying ways, these kids seemed to be more focused than the laid-back Californians I grew up with. Providence had the feel of a college town, something that I had never experienced before. Besides Johnson and Wales, I had discovered the splendid art museum at the Rhode Island School of Design and enjoyed strolling through the grounds of Brown University.

Sue and her friends would also come to visit me as the show came through Hartford, Boston, and New York. A fun break in my routine.

We would maintain our friendship after I left the circus. Much later my graduation from San Francisco State was coming up, and we talked about celebrating with a week in Las Vegas. At first, this idea seemed like a remote possibility, since Las Vegas was a thousand miles from Central California and three thousand miles from the East Coast. After several conversations, our plan began to form. I plowed through final exams, anticipating the reward at the end. Sue, her sister Cheri, and I spent a week at the Flamingo Hilton and had a great time. Dad had kindly loaned me his silver Chrysler LeBaron convertible, the perfect vehicle for such a road trip. At twenty-four, I had reason to celebrate. I had completed what I set out to do, finishing my degree in four years. It was time to kick back for a bit, and then figure out what to do with my life.

We spent a typical touristy week in Vegas. The Flamingo was a perfect location, right on the Strip. In later years, I'd visit Vegas in the summer when it would be unbearably hot, but in January it was pleasant. The three of us took in the sights, strolled through the ornate hotels, and enjoyed downtown, *old school* Las Vegas, and the Liberace Museum. We decided to splurge on a big show at Caesar's Palace and saw Jay Leno, with Bill Medley opening for him.

Our package at the Flamingo hotel included a show. As we downed sloe gin fizzes and watched the variety of performers, I was reminded of choices that we make in life. A juggler appeared, and he was a good one. I realized that I could have reached that level, had I focused on my juggling instead of hitting the books for four years. I suppose it's natural to wonder what might have been.

At the end of our week, Sue and Cheri flew back home while I took the long drive back to Modesto to begin a new life. We figured there would be many more reunion opportunities. I was happy that I had taken this time to celebrate with my friend and her sister.

One day, while working on my master's degree at CSU Stanislaus in Turlock, California, Sue's father left a message on my answering machine. Sue was going through chemotherapy. I was able to reach her on the phone, and she sounded weak. Sue said that she and Cheri cried together because Cheri didn't want to lose her sister. I denied to Sue that there was any danger of that, not thinking of anything else to say. I talked to my parents about the situation, and they urged me to fly back east for a visit, so I did. Sue's father picked me up at my hotel near the Newark airport. We made small talk about some type of historical significance of Linden, New Jersey's role in the Revolutionary War. We drove through the New Jersey Turnpike where Sue had done a stint as a toll taker. In one of her letters, she wrote about a truck driver who asked her to hop in and ride off with him. Sue's father and I arrived at their suburban home, which was comfortably inviting. However, my formerly bubbly friend was bedridden. We sat in her room and talked about nothing in particular.

I was glad that I took a break from my master's thesis to fly over to see my sweet friend. After flying back, Mom and Dad picked me up at the airport and took me out to lunch. Not long before, master clown Lou Jacobs had died, and Stu, my roommate and best friend in college also passed away. I joked, "I have to make new friends. All of mine are dying."

I called Sue from time to time to stay in touch. I thought up excuses to call, like a story I saw a story on *60 Minutes* about shark cartilage treatment for cancer patients. One day when I called, a friend of Sue's answered the phone. She was gone.

Her family and mine stayed in touch for a while. Mom used to run in the New York City Marathon in November. My parents made this an annual vacation, and after Sue's passing, they decided to visit her mother. Once Sue's sister was working sound at a Joe Jackson concert at the San Francisco Civic Center. We met up there and breezed through Chinatown afterward.

My friend Sue saw me through tough times on the road. Her letters were always comforting. Visits when she brought her family and friends lifted my spirits. She was also quite encouraging as I plowed my way through San Francisco State. Sue was always there for me. She's the first person whom I would have called for ideas for this book. I'd tell her that I was working on a memoir about the circus. Sue would have inevitably brought back memories for me to jot down.

On paper we had little to nothing in common. She had grown up in New Jersey, and I in California. Sue was also a social butterfly, while I considered myself more of a loner. Nevertheless, we forged a friendship that will always be a part of me.

14. RUSE

The final stop of the 1984 season was Cleveland. There was a cold bite in the November air, which accompanied the mood in Clown Alley. Some of the clowns had become increasingly embittered that they wouldn't return for the next season. As the youngest clown and one who *was* invited to return, they unfortunately made me a target of their venom.

The break would be short one, just under two weeks, and then it would be time to saddle up for the following season. All of the clowns, whether returning or not, were given the chance to appear in Houston's Thanksgiving Day Parade. In exchange for performing, interested parties would be flown home on Ringling's tab. We'd be put up at the Hyatt Regency plus receive $400 cash for our trouble. The deal sounded good at the time, and I graciously accepted. But the friction with two or three instigators in Clown Alley had come to a head, and I decided to bow out. I fretted for my safety, reasoning that the clowns who were no longer under contract would have nothing to lose. I was leery after being jumped by my boss at Carson & Barnes. What's more, the road was already paved for the next season, and I didn't want to mess anything up. Before a performance, Mr. Holst called me into his office and got right to the point.

"I think it really stinks that you can't go to Houston," he stated. He then suggested that I transfer to the Blue Unit and start fresh.

As a bullheaded nineteen-year-old, I held my ground. I maintained that I had earned the right to stay where I was. I wanted to be part of a new show and visit the big cities on the tour. Playing Chicago and New York would seem like a victory lap, and I was extremely excited about coming to California and having my family see the show.

I was also starting to prepare inwardly for my departure from Ringling. There was a sense of completion in seeing the two routes.

At the time, it seemed that retracing my steps on the rodeo route would be a letdown.

Mr. Holst maintained that my parents would doubtlessly fly out to see me on the road, as they had done in Knoxville and Houston.

Perhaps it was foolish for me to stay in place. Frosty Little, the executive director of clowns, had taken a shine to me at Clown College. He was on the Blue Unit, and surely would have helped me on the road. Mr. Holst claimed Frosty would be delighted to have me in their alley. Frosty had been a calming influence in the manic atmosphere of Clown College. He watched over us as we made our way through that strange course. I think if it were up to Frosty, all Clown College graduates would get contracts. He saw us as human beings, not just fodder for the Ringling machine.

I also observed first-hand Frosty's sense of humanity on the road. I was being bullied by several members of Clown Alley. On a check-in visit he called us together between performances and announced that such hazing wasn't acceptable. As a rookie clown, I found such harassment to be a relatively common practice.

Through it all, Frosty had a laid back, authentic approach. He always got his point across without yelling or threatening. Frosty was an important part of my life and a big reason why I survived Clown College and circus life at a young age. He died in 2010 at age eighty-four. Frosty had achieved the rank of master clown with the Ringling organization, along with Lou Jacobs, Otto Griebling, and Bobby Kaye.

Sometimes I wonder what would have happened, had I switched shows to work with Frosty and the other clowns in the Blue Unit. However, I had made up my mind to stay put.

One more obstacle remained before wrapping up the season. Mr. Holst and I set up a ruse for my safety. We would use the Houston event as a decoy. I pretended I would be participating in the parade, so the offending parties would think they could get their final shots while we were there. It worked like a charm, and I wrapped up the season without too much incident. Clowns rattled off their names in Clown Alley to Mr. Holst and one of the

Ringling officials as they arranged flights from Houston to their hometowns. We maintained the charade, I said I'd be departing to San Francisco.

The season ended and I made it home. I had muddled through and survived my first season on the road with Ringling. I'd have a week and a half to rest and regroup at my parents' house, then fly back for the following season's rehearsals. Mom invited Clarence Dial, my old-time clown mentor, to the house for coffee and her famous fruitcake. Time immemorial, he had been a fixture in the Modesto area in greasepaint and his one-piece costume under the pseudonym *Hokey Pokey*. I agreed with Mom's idea to have Mr. Dial come over for a chat and look through my scrapbook. He kidded me about my volume of newspaper photos of Dolly Jacobs, Lou Jacobs' daughter and an aerialist in the show. That brisk November morning was a chance to reflect on all I'd gone through. Hokey Pokey had been there when being a circus clown was only a dream of mine.

The break also meant our family would spend Thanksgiving together, though I would be in Florida for rehearsals during Christmas. Before I knew it, the time came to return to the show. The rehearsal period would be longer than the previous season because a new show was being put together. Coming back to what were now familiar surroundings, I was able to hit the ground running. This time I felt as if I were moving onto something bigger and better.

When I was a kid, Mom had scolded me about my juggling balls hitting the ceiling of the den while I practiced. I replied to her, "What am I going to tell Ringling Brothers, that I didn't practice because my mother was worried about her ceiling?" Back then the dream of obtaining a berth in Ringling's Clown Alley seemed so distant. It was like a mythical mirage that would only come true under the most remote of circumstances, so it's easy to forgive my teenaged self for thinking the Ringling Brothers and Barnum & Bailey Circus would be a wonderland. Now I knew better, as I mentally and physically prepared for my second year.

15. MAKEOVER

I let the costume designer assigned to me at Clown College take the lead. I figured she knew what she was doing. I thought it wise to bow to her advice, for fear I would be considered rebellious. We collaborated to put together an adequate representation of my clown character. I had a small, elegant red hat, complete with an artificial yellow flower. My wig was yellow. I wore a long-sleeve, striped t-shirt and pants that came to the shin. The shirt featured a costumer's trick of a three-inch Velcro fastener on the neck, used for quick changes. Over that I sported an oversized vest. Colorful socks with huge yellow and red shoes completed the ensemble. I'd reverse the right and left shoes to give my feet room while wheeling around the arena on the contraption stacked three wheels high.

In the seventies and eighties, Ringling had a standard *look* for clowns, which most of us followed. A key to this look was the yak hair wig. The idea was to present a mythical figure. Human hair and skin were not to be seen. I found that it felt comfortable to have my face completely hidden behind clown white. It truly gave me the feeling that I was transforming myself.

As my second year rolled around, I envisioned being a clown with classic European styling. I would keep the shirt and pants but make some changes. I sent home a Victorian style ruffled collar from my menage costume. Mom took it to Dottie's Costume Shop in Ceres, just south of Modesto, so the proprietor could work her magic. It was made of white cheesecloth and decorated with blue ribbon. Dottie confided in my mother that she invented a few swear words while fabricating my new costume piece.

Frosty instructed me on how to take cotton lisle nurse's stockings to make bald caps. I cut out ear holes and hand-sewed reinforcements in them with white thread. Voila! A bald cap. Dottie created a blue satin cummerbund to match the ruff. White Capezio dance shoes with tights underneath were the final touch. Though

I aspired to a new look, I had to bring my wig and oversize clown shoes with me. I hoped the bald cap and white jazz dance shoes would replace my rookie clown implements. However, just in case the *new clown me* was rejected, my original costume was on hand.

I felt comfortable with a simpler, more elegant look. It seemed I was beginning to come into my own. I topped it off with a conical white felt hat. Approval was needed from Kenneth Feld. Chris, the new boss clown, took a Polaroid. We walked together to Mr. Feld's office at the top of the arena. The room had previously been occupied by his father. Mr. Feld said that he had to think about it, taking the photograph from Chris' hand. After a dress rehearsal, he told me to keep the same clown face, but I could have my new costume. I notified Mom, and she went back to Dottie's. Dottie would fabricate a red-trimmed ruff and cummerbund in the same design.

16. ROAD

I savored those ten golden days of lazing around the house in Modesto. Then I returned to the circus as a veteran. The arena in Venice was once the source of angst. Now I had carved out a place for myself.

It felt good to see familiar faces. Father Jack appeared at rehearsal one afternoon. We became friends my first year on the road, and it was always great to see him. However, this time he was there on solemn business. Cindy Dodge, an aerialist on the Blue Unit, had tragically fallen during a practice session, a few hours before the season's final performance. She would die in the hospital. Father Jack came to conduct a memorial service for her. Despite the reason for his presence, he was in his customary positive mood and greeted me warmly.

Cindy Dodge's death was a harsh reminder of the daily dangers faced by aerialists. I had never met her, but as part of the circus "family," I felt it was appropriate for me to be at her memorial. Father Jack conducted his service at the far end of the arena. That part of the building held a special significance for me. It had been a little over a year ago that I had performed in the 1983 Clown College gala performance.

Down the hippodrome track, a couple of young Hungarian acrobats were practicing on a mini trampoline. Mr. Holst shooed them away, and Father Jack began. He reflected on Cindy's career, starting out with Ringling as a showgirl. She eventually moved her way up to dance captain. Over time, she developed her own act.

Conducting the service as a celebration of Cindy's life must have been a challenging task, but Father Jack managed it masterfully. Later, another clown commented to me, "Father Jack really knows his stuff, doesn't he?" I emphatically agreed.

I was also saddened to have my first Christmas away from home. It hit me one evening while we were practicing the entrance and exit from the clown car. The gag had a movie theme, and I played the role of King Kong in a gorilla suit. The seats of the car were removed so numerous clowns could fit inside. We repeatedly entered and exited the Model T, which gave me a chance to think. Christmas had always been special for me and my family. For the first time, I wouldn't be there with them.

The holiday turned out okay. Mr. Feld gave us the day off from rehearsal. Bill Bradley, a self-described *old hoofer,* was one of the three arena choreographers. I had met him at Clown College. Now we had a relationship as colleagues. I referred to him as *Uncle Bill.* He graciously hosted a Christmas party, which soothed the hearts of us who were orphaned for the season. Days passed, and the sadness of being away from home for Christmas dissipated. For a while this would be my home.

Dress rehearsals went well. Kenneth Feld, in Ring Two, proclaimed that the show was almost ready. It felt as if I'd earned my spot, and my self-confidence started to grow. I was beginning to learn my place as a small fish in this very large, colorful, loud, strange pond. Mom sent one of her famous fruitcakes. The lion's share of it was gobbled voraciously by Constantine, the leader of Romania's teeterboard troupe. In addition to his act, acrobats from Bulgaria and Hungary would fill the rings. A smaller acrobat would stand atop the downside of the teeterboard and catapult the fearless, lithe young man or woman into the air. They would be caught in an intricate scaffold of *bottom men* bracing themselves.

Though the hours spent being on call during rehearsals were long, there was a lot of down time. As a typical teenaged boy, I couldn't wait to talk to Mom on the phone about the sixteen showgirls. Innocent flirting became a regular course of events, while I was still too boyish and goofy to be taken seriously as a dating prospect. Instead, these delightful young ladies became buddies, with friendship woven into the midst of preparing for a fresh tour. We chatted in the arena seats, waiting for our call to the floor. Occasionally we did aerobics together to start the day. This was the eighties, after all.

Performers in the show presented their wares to the Ringling brass. Somebody sardonically dubbed this process the *Nuremburg Trials*. At Clown College we learned that rehearsals for the season culminated with a presentation of our material to Mr. Feld. The clown Nuremburg Trials my first season passed rather uneventfully. I had done my job and stayed in place. Because the rehearsal period was short, rookie clowns weren't expected to come up with a large volume of new material. The rehearsal process for the second year of the show's tour was pretty much a brush-up. That was fine with me. I felt that I had enough on my plate, with learning the choreography and adapting to life on the train. This time, I wanted to actively contribute, trying out some material for the show's brass. I was pleased that a gag I presented would be used in come-in, as the audience would file in and take their seats.

Eventually, the 1985 Red Unit of the Ringling Brothers and Barnum & Bailey Circus made its world premiere in the Venice arena. Soon the train was loaded, and it was time to hit the road. First stop, St. Petersburg. As New Year's Eve set, clowns and showgirls hung out around the train. We had the night off and tacitly acknowledged to each other that the journey for the year was underway. It was a bit like a scene from the film *Some Like it Hot*. In the 1959 comedy, a woman's jazz band also travels by rail to a Florida destination.

A couple of the clowns were barbecuing steaks on a hibachi. Some of the showgirls conspired to catch a taxi to ring in the new year at a local disco. I was content to merely sit on the vestibule steps of good old train car #54, my home for another year.

In St. Petersburg, the company also hosted a get-together for the clowns of both units of the circus. I got the chance to chat with Tuba Heatherton, one of the encouraging clowns who had conducted my audition for Clown College in Fresno. That seemed like a lifetime ago. He was happy for me.

I eagerly anticipated the delights of a new season. The show was fresh out of the bandbox, and I felt as if I were, too. I had earned my keep in the circus and marveled at seeing pictures of myself in the souvenir program. The previous year's edition only had a small photograph of my face as a member of the 1983 Clown College class.

We'd perform, pack up, and then the train would rumble off to the next city. I looked forward to our two-month stint at Madison Square Garden in New York that spring. I also kept in mind my homecoming to California that would happen in the summer. Visits to the show from family and friends would be joyous. The Oakland Coliseum Arena was especially pleasing. I had been there as a six-year-old when Mom and Dad took the family to see the California Golden Seals play hockey. I remember little from the game, other than sitting behind Gump Worsley, the goalie for the Minnesota North Stars. Worsley stands out in my mind because he sported his brown seventies sideburns without a mask. Little did I know that after a dozen years, Mom and Dad would be watching *me* on that floor.

The show spent a good amount of time along the West Coast. My sister and other relatives came to performances, visits that lifted my spirits. By now the novelty had worn off, and I felt comfortable as an established clown. Contracts for the next season wouldn't be offered until October, but I had pretty much made up my mind. I'd finish the season at the end of November, return to Modesto, and begin at San Francisco State in January. Before then, however, the California leg of the tour would be filled with family and friends. It was a victory lap of sorts. My twentieth birthday was approaching, and I had begun this endeavor at seventeen. A more conventional life awaited as a college student, but for now, it was time to enjoy circus life, as we passed through Oakland, Fresno, and Anaheim. I remember the anticipation of this homecoming in the blistering heat of Phoenix that July. Soon I'd be home for a while. And then, after wrapping up the tour back east, I'd be home to stay.

Most of my second season was delightful. The longer rehearsal process allowed me to establish myself more as a member of the circus community. In addition to the new relationships I was forming, I was strengthening bonds from my first year.

17. FAREWELL

Like Forrest Gump, I was in the right place at the right time to witness something extraordinary. My second and last year on the road was the season Ringling unveiled *The Living Unicorn*, for better or worse. The show made international news. Management never provided us with the story of the one-horned goat and for good reason. A reporter from *The New York Post,* whom I made up as a guest clown, grilled me for information on it. I reported to Mr. Holst promptly that I claimed I knew nothing about the *mythical creature*, and he replied, "Smart boy." This would prove to be just one of my many memorable moments in New York City.

The 1985 tour brought me to the Big Apple for the first time. The venerable discotheque Studio 54 and *A Chorus Line,* Broadway's longest-running show, were in full swing. Ben Vereen, host of the TV special of circus highlights that year, gave us tickets to see his Broadway show, *Grind.* It was extra special for Mom and Dad to visit me in New York. Mr. Vereen was a favorite of Mom's, and she was truly thrilled when he rode in on an elephant during a rally for the unicorn.

After two months of performances, it was time to finish up in Manhattan. The Tony Awards show at the Schubert Theater coincided with the night we closed at Madison Square Garden. Around the time those three goddesses from *Dream Girls* presented an award on my little Sony black and white, my buddy Michael and I had decided to make a final trek to Broadway. By the time we got there, the ballyhoo was over. A single white limousine was waiting outside the stage door. We ducked into a dive bar on Times Square to down one more Long Island Iced Tea, sadly toasting our departure. Michael and I hurried to catch the subway back to Queens; we'd truly be in a fix if the circus train went on to Philadelphia without us. Playing New York was one reason for my sense of completion with Ringling after those two years.

One night, after the show, close to the end of the 1985 season, I announced in the shower room that I had been accepted to San Francisco State. My fellow clowns cheered and congratulated me. Banter between myself and others shifted to my academic future.

The time to go home crept closer. While working out the logistics of shipping my gear, I got acquainted with a purchasing agent for the show. I don't remember his name, but do recall his laid back, confident manner. A frequent smile revealed teeth which looked as if they had been worked over with a rattail file. Somehow, he had heard about my fight at Carson & Barnes and announced to another Ringling hand that I had "mopped up the midway with the guy." Mr. Holst had also acknowledged my scuffle from months past, and I asked him how he knew about it. He replied, "The circus world isn't that big, Andy."

The season wound down, while Mr. Holst and I continued our banter behind the curtain. As in the previous year, he casually mentioned the upcoming season. However, this time I said that I wasn't coming back. Mr. Holst thought it was strange; I had been through so much. Nevertheless, he respected my decision and understood that it was important for me to get an education. When I asked him if he thought college was ready for me, he joked, "Andy, you might set the American education system back a hundred years."

Along with Mr. Holst, Father Jack had been a good friend to me throughout my two years at Ringling. With my final season drawing toward a close, he kindly told me that the alley would be losing a good clown.

I wanted to receive a college education and knew I'd have to leave the circus to get it. I had done what I had set out to do with Ringling. Still, as the end of the season drew near, I understood that it was also hard to leave something that I grew to love so much.

The bite of autumn accompanied us as we hugged the East Coast to wrap up the season. I would leave. It was time.

Fear of the unknown crept up, and I started placing undue pressure on myself. At eighteen it seemed I set impossibly high standards when I signed my first Ringling contract. How could I follow that?

Back in my first year on the road, one of the clowns announced it was his twentieth birthday. Old Duane the clown proclaimed that once the teen years are over, life gets easier. In the movie *Platoon,* a soldier celebrates with Charlie Sheen as he gets ready to leave Vietnam, proclaiming, "It's all gravy." This meant that he had survived something so momentous, getting through the rest of his life would be easy.

I haven't found things to be so simple. I had a sense of being a survivor in subsequent years. I learned that old rites of passage would give way to new ones. Two years with Ringling gave me the opportunity to live in a box, both literally and figuratively. My entire set of responsibilities consisted of preparing myself for performances and performing in them. All expectations were laid out for me. Within a few weeks I had learned everything I would need to know. Arena choreography was down pat, as well as the gags I had appeared in. Rent and utilities on the train were part of our compensation package. Outside of an occasional refill of my make-up, my only regular expense was for food. I always made more than enough money on the road. In fact, I usually saved half of my pay. Time management wasn't an issue. The only concern was being in greasepaint and behind the curtain before the performance began.

I was nervous about entering the world of term papers and final exams. Up to this point, I had been a lackluster student. Mom warned me as I was getting ready for college, that I hadn't studied in a long time. She knew all too well that I could be terribly hard on myself.

On the train in Seattle one night, my buddy Michael and I were flipping through the TV channels and landed on a local talk show. The guest was a jovial Alan Hale Jr., who had played *the Skipper* on

Gilligan's Island. He stated that for a while he had a successful restaurant that traded on his name. Then he eloquently described its demise, saying that he let it go "on the crest of a wave."

I heard this poetic, burly man speak and realized that the days remaining in the season were getting fewer. I started to picture my leaving, also, on *the crest of a wave.* It didn't turn out that way. I would feel more as if I locked the office door behind me and turned in my keys.

18. RETURN

My youthful exuberance and occasional brash manner rubbed some people the wrong way. This was especially true with non-performers I'd encounter, such as the elephant handlers. I watched over my shoulder as the end of the season approached. Like my situation at Carson & Barnes, I was anxious to get out of there for my safety. After the final performance, I didn't bother showering and just used cold cream and a towel to remove my greasepaint. I shook hands with some of the clowns. Duane Thorpe, who by now was a three-decade veteran of Clown Alley, sported a navy-blue suit and open-neck shirt. He'd be flying to a home he purchased in Spain, through saving his salary as a clown. Two seasons later, I came back to the show in Oakland, and he was selling programs. Some eight years after that, while I was working in Mexico at a resort, Mom sent me a copy of Duane's obituary from the *San Francisco Chronicle.*

As the 1985 season ended, an impromptu party took place back-stage at the arena in East Rutherford, New Jersey. As with every season, some would be returning, some would be leaving. I was in no mood to stick around for the celebration.

Because I was on the East Coast, I decided to take a week's vacation in New York City. I had grown to love it there. Michael and I rode the Long Island Railroad to Manhattan together. He'd catch a plane home for a break in Morgantown, West Virginia, and then return for the following season. He said, "You be wonderful," and we hugged. My friend Wayne was in *A Chorus Line,* and we caught each other's shows when we could. He graciously put me up in his Manhattan apartment for a week, as I began to decompress. It was a perfect way to end the tour. I went to a salon and got a massage, facial, manicure, and pedicure. Wayne's roommate, Joel, and I attended *Cavalleria Rusticana* and *Pagliacci* at the New York Metropolitan Opera, and my lifelong love for this art form was born. Knocking around town in New York for a few days was fun but soon it was time to fly home and regroup in Modesto before beginning life as a college student.

I was ready for the next phase of my life, but there was a sense of loss. Dorothy knew that it was time to exit Oz but was still sad about leaving her friends. I'd have a few weeks in the cool winter months of Modesto to putter around, and eventually get to campus and hit the books. Mom said to me, "There's nothing as *over* as the circus."

After my return, I was in the car with Mom and Dad one night. Neil Diamond's song, *I Am, I Said,* came on the radio. The lyrics express how he was a frog, dreamed of being a king, and then became one.

I felt like a frog again, flopping about at home. Mom and Dad were worried and sat me down in the kitchen for a talk. Mom asked what was wrong. She acknowledged that I had been riding the circus high for some time. At twenty, I considered myself a has-been.

I spent some time juggling in the backyard, but it wasn't the same. I knew that I was embracing something new and still had some trouble letting go of the past. My journey on the road was complete. Now it was time to put myself into student mode, which was really a first for me. In high school I had bided my time and made a marginal effort. Soon it would be time to get serious about academics.

I was contacted by some of the local media. Fred Schwartz from *The Modesto Bee* had written a story on me when I was at Clown College. This time I drove to the paper's offices to have my picture taken. Paul, a high school buddy of mine, worked as a disc jockey at a local radio station, *Sunny 102*. He arranged for me to come in for an interview on the station's morning program, which was quite enjoyable. Hindsight is twenty-twenty, and I now see myself at that time as a pretentious know-it-all. Nevertheless, both newspaper and radio interviewers listened patiently as I pontificated on the triumphs and trials of life on the road.

After all these years, there are still times when I instinctively tell myself that I need to perform in some way for others. Day in and day out, whether as a Clown College student or working clown, I was in greasepaint a large portion of my waking hours. Something *more*, it seemed, was expected of me from strangers in the audiences. Now, sitting alone with a cup of coffee in a public place, I still have a heightened appreciation for my privacy.

Change occurs, for better and worse. On January 28, 1986, the morning my mother brought me to move in at San Francisco State, the space shuttle Challenger exploded shortly after take-off. Kristi McAuliffe, a teacher, and all the astronauts on board were killed. The event put a damper on move-in day. I remember watching from the TV in the basement of the student union. At first, in the clear Florida sky, the white rocket ship appeared to be going fine. Then a yellow flash appeared, like the beginning of a fireworks display, and the craft was annihilated. The television kept replaying the explosion, to the horror of the crowd of viewers. I was reminded that no one day is perfect.

And so, I went back to being *just a person*. This time, a college student. I was nervous about sharing a room with somebody. My prior roommate experience at Clown College with Brent was a strained one. Unfortunately, the relationship I had with my first-term college roomy had even more friction. Tony was a nice enough guy. I suppose it would have been a good idea to get along with him, instead of scolding his untidiness. Unkindly, I referred to him as *Tony the Pig* around campus.

I didn't know what I was going to do with my life and figured college would show me the way. For hours I had pored over the schedule of classes for the Spring, 1986 semester. The choices were overwhelming. Finally, I decided on a less challenging schedule for my first term. Early success in higher education was important to me, and I wanted to ease into my new life as a scholar. I used the cakewalk classes I had chosen, such as an introductory acting class and a course in public speaking, to build my GPA and confidence.

I made some friends on campus. A guy from the dorms was assistant director of the school's production of Shakespeare's *A Comedy of Errors* and cast me as an extra. A large part my first term in college was fun and light, something I needed at that stage of my life. I called home frequently, and it pleased Mom that I was happy.

There's a wonderful safety net in college, especially when one lives in the residence halls. Hopefully, the young adult emerges from this sheltered compound with some wisdom under his belt.

It was time to focus on my academics, and life in the dorms made this simple. I could eat, sleep, and breathe school, in a literal sense. With Ringling I had become familiar with throwing myself into my work. Now my *work* was school. I knew that I had it made. Elbow grease became the primary ingredient for success, as my fingers became more and more adept at tapping out term papers on my electric Olympia typewriter. College became a sanctuary. Meals were provided, and I didn't need a car.

As an undergrad, I discovered the magic of padding my transcript through taking courses Credit/No Credit, like *Understanding Politics*. Turns out I would have earned a B-. Not a bad grade, but it would have prevented me from graduating summa sum laude three and a half years later. Technically I earned straight A's my first term. This was something I had never done before, even in sixth grade, when Stanislaus Elementary switched to letter grades. Summer came around in a hurry. Other than an incident with a fire extinguisher on my residence hall floor, I had a successful term. I truly didn't know what to do with myself during vacation time and didn't want to spend it in Modesto. An acquaintance said her family had a room for rent in San Leandro, a suburban community in the East Bay. I got a job at the Oakland UPS hub and began ineptly loading trucks. Mercifully, I was placed on *small sort*, earning money for rent and food by placing little packages into plastic bags. The hub was next to the Oakland Coliseum Arena. Seeing the building was a daily reminder of what I had left behind. I had worked inside as a clown the previous summer, but it seemed a lifetime ago.

It was hard enough to *get* the job in the circus and survive while there. What now? Where does a clown go? I couldn't wait for the fall semester to begin. Life would hold a new magic, different from in the circus. San Francisco State University is known for its creative arts program, which adds to the ambiance of the facility. It's easy to walk about campus and see a dozen would-be Shakespeares, Fellinis, or Oliviers. That's the beauty of youth.

I eventually got on a roll with my higher education experience and began legitimizing my time there by bringing home good grades in solidly academic classes.

To date I've never again experienced the sense of fairness, rhyme, and reason of being a college undergraduate. There were no office politics or pecking order. I busted my hump each term and received high grades to show for it. I focused on my academics, and the rest took care of itself.

My circus experience served me well in college. There's no doubt I did much better academically than I would have if I had gone straight to San Francisco State after high school. Ringling taught me that great things can happen when I apply myself. It was an unusual springboard into adult life. I captured some of my experiences on the road and six sociology credits in a lengthy term paper I called *Tears of a Clown*. The 1986 retrospective would be the seed for this book. No, Smokey Robinson's representatives never called to accuse me of lifting the title.

In an orientation for new SF State students, I described college as a time of picking and choosing what kind of adult I wanted to become. Like a *salad bar*. I believe the fact that I stayed away from drugs enhanced my college experience. It may never have been fashionable to make such a statement, especially in the *Just Say No* days of Nancy Reagan, and it was going on all around me, but something always told me to stay away. I was finding out that life itself was enough of a challenge without these additional burdens.

Reflecting on those days, George Bernard Shaw's proclamation that *youth is wasted on the young* keeps haunting me. Gradually, as Mom put it, I was getting *real world lessons*. Foolishly, I figured I was now Superman at twenty, having paid my dues, found myself, and fulfilled my destiny. One of the great things about the college years is that failures, mishaps, and screw-ups can often occur without any ill consequences. I started out with all A's after my first term, though my academic load wasn't a heavy one. But during my second semester, I discovered that I had a lot more to accomplish with my academics, as I came up scratching for a B in both geology and freshman composition. Ringling had given me the opportunity to do something out of the ordinary, but that was over. I had pursued excellence at Clown College, got lucky, and got to go on the road as a result. Again, as a student, it was time to work toward the extraordinary.

Meanwhile, my parents made sure to keep me grounded during this time, as they had done throughout my life. As a child, I recall watching *The Wonderful World of Disney,* a Sunday Night ritual in our home. Walt Disney appeared in an interview from the archives. A familiarly dashing Walt sported his signature pencil-thin mustache and blazer with wide lapels. I asked my father what he thought it was like for Disney to master such an organization. Dad pragmatically maintained, "It's a job," like running any business. Mom, too, helped me keep perspective while visions of show business danced in my head. Years after *The King* was gone, we were watching a rerun of Elvis' *Aloha from Hawaii* concert, universally recognized as his apex before the long downward spiral. He had perfectly groomed, long hair with sideburns, and chiseled, tanned features. Elvis sported vibrant yellow and red leis over a white bejeweled jumpsuit. Between songs Mom, Dad, and I discussed the sadness of his eventual demise. Mom said thoughtfully, "See what happens when you take yourself too seriously?" She wasn't the only one to spout such wisdom. My roommate Brent had told me that I was taking Clown College too seriously. Tim Holst had told me I was taking my experience on the road too seriously. I like to think that with Mom's Elvis statement, in my early twenties, this notion was beginning to sink in.

I loved being a college kid and, even back then, sensed that I would always cherish this time in my life. Mom and Dad were pleased that I had gotten on a roll with my coursework, and I eventually settled on a major in broadcasting. While home from college, I had gotten acquainted with Bob Fenton, who had made his fortune as owner of a string of radio stations. Out of the blue, he asked me if I wanted a job. I was to report to a talk radio station in Santa Barbara, to join the sales force. I borrowed Dad's car and took the long, leisurely drive, not knowing what to expect. The station's general manager, Bill Johnson, was larger than life. I figured the burly man to be in his sixties. Grey cropped hair gave way to a big, pock-marked face. Large, gapped teeth showed through an expression that was inscrutable as either a smile or sneer. A meaty hand gripped mine, and we sat to talk in his office. An open neck shirt and cheap light blue flannel blazer accompanied his plain talk. In contrast with his unimpressive attire, Bill sported a pinkie ring on his left hand, diamonds in the shape of a dollar sign. He chose to clear the air by insisting that he wasn't a *yes man* for Fenton, and that he could hire whom he wanted. His response was predictable when I let him know I wanted to complete my degree. This wouldn't be a summertime gig. I knew he'd want a long-term commitment. I questioned why he would want me for this job, considering I had no experience. He smiled, winked, and responded, "You're a pretty good kid." Bill advised I take three days and think about it, to go be a bum on the beach for a while, then get back to him.

I left the office in the afternoon heat, knowing I wouldn't need three days. I knew right then. It was a five-hour drive back to Modesto, so I decided to spend the night. I drove around and found a cheap hotel in nearby Carpinteria. Turned out Dad had played football on the field behind the building when he was in high school. I called home, and Mom supported my decision to turn down the job. I think she was more elated than she let on. The June sun seemed to stay in the sky forever as I holed up in the small room. On the TV, Oliver North huddled with his counsel over the Iran-Contra affair. I drove back to the station the next morning to announce my decision to Bill. He wasn't there, and there was no telling when he'd be in. I was an average boy in Modesto until I was seventeen. The circus experience, until twenty, took its logical course from Carson & Barnes, Clown College, and then Ringling's traveling show. Then came time to hit the books at San Francisco State. In due time, life would become more complicated, with career issues and bills to pay. I still wanted to be a college kid for a while.

19. CONFUSION

By 1987, I was settled in quite well at San Francisco State. As a Clown College graduate, I had been invited to participate in a twentieth anniversary celebration, hosted by Dick Van Dyke. It was indeed tempting, especially to a huge fan of his. However, I was on a roll with my academics and didn't want to miss a week of school. Also, as Mom and I discussed later, I wasn't emotionally ready to return.

I put on the greasepaint a handful of times during my college years, but without the circus, the magic wasn't there for me. My sometime girlfriend Liz and I came up with the idea for working on a comedy juggling and mime act for *Pier 39*. The tourist attraction on Fisherman's Wharf featured street performers. We were taking a comedy writing class and figured the development of an act would be a way to kill two birds with one stone. Both of us got an A in the class but never performed our show at the pier.

Reminders of my circus past cropped up as I came close to completing my bachelor's degree. Ruthie Chaddock, who taught in my Clown College class, was still working for Ringling in public relations. I was serving as an intern at a local TV station and invited her to be a guest on a talk show. We chatted over old times, and I wondered if I would ever be a part of that world again. I also dropped by a downtown audition for Clown College, and it was only natural to feel nostalgia for the good old days.

After three years, it seemed the party of college was over. I looked at it now as merely a place to finish my degree and build my future. A highlight of my waning undergrad experience was *Symbolic Logic,* a loophole course that fulfilled the mathematics requirement. Way back in my first semester I had stored away this information, and now I used it as a trump card to graduate on time. Test taking anxiety was a frequent familiar burden, and a bonus was that I wouldn't be required to take the university's math exam if I completed this course at San Francisco City College. I was beginning to find out that the absurd tenets of bureaucracy can sometimes work in my favor. I had only four classes before graduation. The other three were *Analysis of the Public Arts, History of the United States Since 1865,* and *Holistic Health: Eastern Perspectives.* Each course had its own challenges. Then again, none of them were rocket science. Only one more semester, four months, until I graduated. I was no longer living on campus and had a dissatisfying semester renting a room in Colma, fairly close to school. I needed a place to live and found out that a bartender was renting a room in his apartment. It was by the beach.

Unfortunately, my two years on the road did nothing to alleviate my fear of mathematics. Real world geometrical applications came back to haunt me when I was relegated to help hang the rigging for the flying trapeze. If motivated, I could have put time and effort into deciphering the daily tangle of cables and pulleys, but it really didn't matter to me.

It *did* matter, however, when I was learning Symbolic Logic. Plain and simple, an A in that course was required to graduate *summa cum laude.* I met with other students for extra study sessions. I taped and reviewed lectures on microcassettes. I met with the professor to review concepts during office hours. I hired a tutor who was recommended by the professor. My life that September through December became wrapped around success in that class. I made it through the final exam but had no idea what the result would be. We'd be notified by mail.

I had been at my Uncle George's house six years prior, when I got the call to go on the road with Ringling. He happened to be visiting us in Modesto to mark another milestone in my life when the notice arrived in the mail. I was assigned the grade of A in Symbolic Logic. However, I will forever be suspect that kind empathy on the professor's part, observing my overwhelming devotion to his course, played a part in the determination of this mark. With this grade, summa cum laude was in the bag.

116

The holiday season was extra celebratory that year because I had obtained my degree. What to do next? Four years later, as when I left the circus, I felt depleted. But this time, I didn't know where to go. Too bad there was no *halfway house* for recent college graduates. I had been so focused on the academics (as well I should have been), that it was hard to think beyond final exams. By the time the term was done, I was physically and emotionally drained. In shame I called Mom and Dad, confessing that I had driven Dad's truck down the steep cement driveway outside of my apartment on Balboa Street and got stuck. Somehow, I got out and made it to Modesto.

No, I didn't conduct myself like Dustin Hoffman's character in *The Graduate*. A *Mrs. Robinson,* in my case, was nowhere to be found. I was just as confused as his character, however. Mom and Dad had some sanding and painting on the awning above the patio for me to do, and I would go from there.

I had nine different W-2 forms in 1990, and I even had gone to bartender's school. That year, I also began my master's degree in Communication at California State University, Stanislaus. The campus is in Turlock, a half-hour drive south of Modesto. I had grown accustomed to the structure of school and felt lost without it. What's more, I figured a graduate degree could always come in handy. Mom, Dad, and I hadn't established a steadfast deadline, but the end of 1990 also marked a logical benchmark for getting a place of my own. At year's end I landed on a job selling commercial time at KJOY, a radio station in Stockton.

I had never been further removed from the world of the circus, than I was in the first half of my twenties. I figured that time in my life was buried and gone forever. Back home in Modesto after college, my girlfriend at the time, named Tina, confided that her parents didn't trust me because I had been in the circus. We had been apart for half a year, while she worked at a radio station in Paris, Texas. I had time to think, away from her and away from my parents, in my first apartment near the University of the Pacific.

As far as I know, there's no such thing as a twelve-step program for circus addiction. At seventeen, it was in my blood. Possibly it got there even before that, when Mom first took me to Circus Vargas a decade prior. Lady Circus again whispered in my ear, at a Bentley Brothers show on the university's football field. This was the same show that baboon trainer Irvin Hall and I had attended back in 1984. The circus also had some Romanian acrobats that I knew from my days in Ringling. I remembered that the leader of the troupe, Constantine, loved the fruitcake my mom had sent for the show to sample in rehearsals. However, I didn't bother to find them afterward. By now I had gone to college and got a "real" job. In my mind there was no need to go into *Remember me?* mode.

As in the song *Don't Cry out Loud,* all that was left behind was some sawdust and glitter. After the show, I scooped up some sawdust and a tiny scrap of discarded shiny blue thread from somebody's circus costume that were left behind. I mailed it to Tina. Some people would understand this gesture, symbolic of an aspect of my life that would always be a part of me. She didn't.

At twenty-six, it seemed that I was finding a place for myself. I was on a steady course with my job. The three-month probationary period was behind me, and I was gaining momentum with clients. In addition, I was working in the broadcast industry, which related to my college major. Tina was planning to come back to California.

I can't blame the circus for breaking us up, but it didn't help. Our contrasting views on the topic was just one item on a laundry list of differences we had. We met during the frenetic year after my graduation. Both of us were board operators at KASH, a newly formed talk radio station in Modesto. Our on again, off again relationship was on hiatus when Tina applied for the job in Texas. We got back together before she left and decided to wait for each other.

After her return to California, we were treated to box seats at Circus Vargas, an ad client of mine. I also got to be guest ringmaster. My involvement in the circus this time was quite tangential. Still, I was excited to be back, however briefly, in this atmosphere. Tina was hot and bored on that balmy June evening under the big top and wanted to leave early. She asked why our conversations frequently circled around to the circus. I said, "I know that if I went back, you wouldn't go with me." My life, with my job, was becoming more conventional. Yet in the backstretch of my twenties, I still wanted to maintain the potential for adventure.

I wasn't ready to let go of my dreams but was adopting a new sense of responsibility. The beginning of a circus tour and the first term in pursuit of a college degree had both carried a sense of wonder. However, when the newness wore off and the real work had commenced, grit to see the experience through took hold. Through solitude I found a means to adapt and work through transitions, to face upcoming challenges.

It wasn't my life's ambition to sell radio time. However, it did serve as a vehicle to get out of my parents' house and establish a place to live on my own. Also, I figured it was an effective way to put my broadcasting degree to use. I suppose I learned a thing or two about life from my chain-smoking, blunt-speaking boss named Al. Discussing how to prospect for clients, Al proclaimed, "If you throw enough %@*& against the wall, something is bound to stick."

20. MORE

Leaving KJOY wasn't a particularly smart move, as I was beginning to come into my own as a salesman. At a breakfast for local businesses, I met a lady who managed Delta Charter, a tour bus company. She wanted to hire a tour guide, so I interviewed and got the job. I can't put my finger on the reason why that job didn't take; it just wasn't to be. After that I snatched up a job at a Shell gas station and found an apartment in Turlock. Time to start over again. It had seemed a logical choice to move to Turlock and plow through my MA program, doing whatever was necessary to support myself along the way.

My studio apartment had a simple functionality. The door opened into a small kitchen. A board extended from the wall, propped on two wooden legs. This served as my desk. I brought my futon over from my old apartment in Stockton. Eventually I would add a wooden frame that would convert into a sofa. The grey wall of the building had the words *FAR EAST APARTMENTS* cut out in white, wooden, faux Asian-style characters like the ones on signs of midlevel Chinese restaurants. Several college students lived there. Behind the laundry room there was a small pool, where I'd occasionally take a dip on hot summer afternoons. A late middle-aged lady lived near the pool and could frequently be seen in her living unit, sitting upright in a chair, reading books. She was surrounded by plants.

A stroll across the lawn of the apartment complex, and then another across Crowell Road, and the next lawn meant my feet were officially on campus. There was a small amphitheater, where I would eventually participate in the commencement ceremonies. I didn't mind the half mile walk to the communications department. One would think that they could come up with a more original name than the *Classroom Building*. It was nice to avoid the drive to school.

I talked to Bob Fenton, who had connected me several years before to the radio station in Santa Barbara. This time, Mr. Fenton suggested I contact Bob Salmon, who ran KMIX, a country station in Turlock. I interviewed and was hired. Cold calling on businesses was familiar to me now; I had done it successfully in Stockton.

The plan was to work full time selling commercials at KMIX and gradually inch toward my master's degree. However, one day my advisor called me into his office. He offered me a one-semester graduate assistantship. I would teach a course in public speaking and receive a small salary. I talked Bob Salmon into letting me keep my sales job. I would be teaching on Tuesdays and Thursdays from 8:00-9:30 AM, which would naturally cut into my sales. In addition, I kept the coursework for my master's, which was why I was in Turlock in the first place. Predictably, my fragmented attention caused me to be unsuccessful in any of these endeavors. By summertime I was worn out and frustrated.

Eventually, I knew it was time to leave the station; they didn't have to fire me. Again, I was to salvage my life. I started to pick up hours at the campus food service facility. Dad needed help from time to time delivering eggs, and there was an opening to load trucks. My coursework crept along.

By now I was on the tail end of my master's program. It was late summer, and Ringling had made its way through San Francisco. Michael, my best friend from Clown Alley, had rejoined the show. I met with him and a few others for dinner on their night off. As a circus civilian, I crossed the Bay Bridge in the pleasant August twilight with the top down on my green convertible Volkswagen Rabbit. I chatted with a married couple, fellow Ringling vets. One used to be a clown, and the other was a showgirl. They were now working at the San Francisco School of Circus Arts, which featured flying trapeze instruction. I think of Al Pacino in *The Godfather, Part 3,* lamenting to his wife, "Just when I thought I was out, they pull me back in."

To sit contentedly on my perch like a parakeet, then pull a lithe acrobat from the air… Way back when signing my contract for my second year at Ringling, I had foolishly asked Kenneth Feld if I could climb up the swing and work out with the Flying Españas. Predictably he denied my request, saying that it wouldn't be possible because of insurance issues. Strangely, it took my getting out of the circus world to begin my dream of catching. There's no feeling like grabbing someone from the air, guiding their backswing, and then releasing them back to the bar, the timing just right. Eventually I would get there. For now, I was wrapping up my master's and had time to pursue what was then a new hobby.

I holed up in Turlock and finished my degree. I recognize that I could have approached this project with a more positive attitude. Instead, I grew restless and agitated. Each section of my thesis had to be approved by a committee of three people. I would turn in a section and wait. I found that there was really no way to speed the plow.

Strangely, something continued calling me to the trapeze, though the drive to the San Francisco School of Circus Arts was two hours long. I got out to the facility occasionally. The rest of the time I was motivated to pump weights in the gym on campus. I didn't know how, where, or why, but sensed that trapeze, at some point, would play a role in my future. I dared to dream of entering the ring with my troupe.

Mom said, "You're awful old," when I mentioned this aspiration. I think I used the words, "Wouldn't it be neat?" It would take me a decade to finally work that notion out of my system.

I eventually completed my thesis. When it was over, I truly didn't know what to do next. Sound familiar? I kept my subsistence employment. At this time in my life, I aspired to go on to Florida State University and pursue a doctorate in Communication. It didn't hurt that FSU had a renowned circus school, where I could also continue to train on the trapeze.

I decided to go through the commencement ceremony for my master's at CSU Stanislaus. Mom, Dad, and my sister came, and it was fun. Professionally, though, I was still in limbo. While in my gown, Linda, my boss at the campus kitchen, gave me a congratulatory hug. She reminded me that I was scheduled to work at a catering event the following day.

The familiar sense of angst began to set in on what to do next. Gratefully, frugal living and a little luck prevented me from student debt. However, my nest egg was pretty much depleted. I pondered what to do with my fresh start. Would trapeze figure into my future? As a beginner, I didn't yet allow myself to think too seriously about establishing a career in a troupe. What's more, I started catching very late in life, and the possibility was already remote. Would I pursue a doctorate, and in turn become a professor of communication studies? Would I go back into radio sales? I had a knack for it, though it was never my dream job. I was open to just about anything.

On a whim, I wrote to Kenneth Feld, Ringling's owner, asking him about the possibility of putting me to work for his organization. A few days later I got a call from one of the marketing vice presidents. He would be my new boss. We talked for a while, and he told me that I would be flying to Las Vegas to begin my career as a promoter for the circus. I was beside myself with joy. I moved out of the Far East Apartments, packing my belongings, and cleaning the space carefully. I leisurely loaded the white panel truck, the same one that I used for moving out four and a half years prior in San Francisco. On the television there was another large white vehicle on screen, a Bronco. O.J. Simpson was making his futile effort to flee the police.

Mom and Dad would let me stay at home, while I packed up my life for this new adventure. I bought a snappy white and blue plaid Bill Blass suit. I had little time off since beginning my master's thesis and decided, somewhat randomly, to take a drive to spend a couple days in Monterey. I figured time looking at the bay would be a good way to wrap my head around the upcoming task. I eagerly anticipated my second tour of duty with Ringling. This time I reasoned that I was older and wiser, with two degrees under my belt. At twenty-eight, it seemed that I had perspective and direction. I had loved the company since first being exposed to it at seventeen. This was where I wanted and needed to be. A fresh start.

I caught the plane and it touched down in an hour. I had been to Las Vegas four and a half years prior, to celebrate the completion of my undergrad degree with my friend Sue and her sister Cheri.

This time I was in Las Vegas on business. I allowed myself to believe that the circus was my destiny. Dockers and an open neck shirt would have done just fine for my arrival, but I insisted on being decked out in my new suit. I arrived at the arena and waited. In 1985, the show hadn't played Las Vegas, so it was a new venue for me. The promoters were assigned a midsize conference room with a big screen TV mounted on the wall. A World Cup soccer game wound down. Someone switched to MTV. It wasn't blasting but loud enough to provide ample white noise for the busy work to be done. The video for Green Day's *Paranoid* was featured. The guitarist, bass player, and drummer banged out their tune in the setting of a hospital ward. I questioned myself about the taste of placing the drummer in a wheelchair. My own mindset would mirror that of the serenading trio, who were relating their angst in general about their surroundings.

The smart thing would have been to keep my mouth shut and stay out of the way. However, I failed to hide my overwhelming zeal for this position. Even when I was a teenager working as a clown, I had my eyes on a job like this one. I remember, between performances, proclaiming to my mom from an arena payphone that I had wanted to go into management with the Ringling organization. A decade had passed. I kept this idea in the back of my head as I went through my undergrad degree, master's, and various jobs along the way. Foolishly, I was in the mindset of a soldier landing on the beaches of Normandy on D-Day. The wonder boy, not yet thirty, who would save the circus. Sad but true, the job wouldn't be about my hitting the ground running. Come to think of it, I never would find out exactly what my duties were.

My first days there, I figured, were an opportunity to become oriented to the business world of the circus. I wasn't given any real responsibilities. I'd wander the arena corridor with a two-way radio, chatting up the concessionaires. I was reminded of the small-ness of the circus world while meeting up with Lolis and Alex, old buddies of mine from Carson & Barnes. They were now married, minding a souvenir stand. Lolis knew me as a seventeen-year-old, wearing grubby clothes around the big top. She appeared im-pressed that I was now in business clothes.

I'd be instructed to redundantly give the red-jacketed ushers instructions on a job that they already knew how to perform. I'd drop by for a chat in Clown Alley. Although this was the Blue Unit and I had been on the red, I was acquainted with several of the clowns from years past. It didn't matter to me that I wasn't given any real responsibilities; I figured that my duties would grow with time. I was elated to be in this world again. Jerry Lewis came to the show, and it was a thrill to talk to him. I asked him about the circus movie he had made with Dean Martin, and he replied that it was before I was born.

I was flown to San Diego to do pretty much the same thing. More babysitting with ushers. More hanging out and chatting up the circus personnel. More walking around with a two-way radio, looking important. The V.P. who hired me said that he wanted to talk. I sat down, and he said that this "isn't working out." After ten days as a promoter, I was fired.

It seemed that a world I loved so passionately didn't love me back. Through my undergraduate work and grad school, I always figured that Ringling would be open to me, should I ever want to return. No longer.

I don't know how long my boss had been planning to have *the talk* with me. The forethought was long enough to have a one-way plane ticket to San Francisco in hand. I was instructed to take the rental car back to the motel, stay the night, and fly home the next morning, but I felt no need to drive. I gathered my few belongings from backstage at the Sports Arena and found a brown paper bag to put them in. Then I walked that sad mile back to the motel. The next scene had eerie similarities to the morning that I wasn't accepted to go on the road from Clown College. On the phone Mom suggested I go ahead to the airport and arrange for an earlier flight. Southwest Airlines was in the height of its marketing tool of promoting humor. The flight attendant on the hour-long trip engaged in her vaudevillian act, as I became even more miserable. As she quipped about the pilot being a member of the Hair Club for Men and imitating a train engine while the plane was taking off, I just wanted to get home.

I was broken. This was how Pete Best must have felt when the Beatles replaced him with Ringo Starr. Mom and Dad wisely decided that I should regroup quickly. They sensed if I started moping around the house, it could become a miserable, prolonged habit. We agreed that I'd take a couple days, then figure out what to do next.

A storybook career about a boy becoming a clown, getting educated, then working his way through the business end of the organization. Over lunch at the Hard Rock Café in Las Vegas, an enthusiastic publicist from San Diego named Jack had mentioned that this was a great story. Whatever the reason, it wasn't to be.

Time heals wounds, and I've moved on through necessity. However, to my dying day I'll know that given a chance, I would have shined as a promoter for the circus. I don't claim to have had a superior intellectual aptitude that would deem me a wunderkind in marketing. But I will always know in my heart that my fanatical devotion to an entity that I so cherished could have had dynamic results.

21. PORTABLE

Mom was commuting to San Francisco at the time. We figured it would be a good idea for me to drive in with her and look for work there. Within a few weeks, I settled on Harry Mason, a designer jewelry store on Pier 39. It was time to build from the bottom up, again. I rented a studio apartment downtown and made the daily walk to the job, over Nob Hill to the wharf. It was a hard fall, but I landed on my feet. Thankfully, I started catching on the trapeze again. I came back to the San Francisco School of Circus Arts, to the familiar swing. It was time to pick up where I left off as a catcher. I stretched in my tights, enjoying what was a homecoming of sorts.

I was gradually piecing my life together again. I became a regular at the circus school, which was run by veterans of a well-known resort company. (Hint: The name combines a word beginning with C, synonymous with organization, and started off the coast of the Mediterranean Sea.) The company had devised a circus wing, which included instruction and performance at several of its fine resorts. This organization would play into my future on the trapeze, or so I thought.

My mindset was to catch to the point where I would be adept enough to apply for a troupe. I sensed that if I wanted to move to the next level as a trapeze catcher, I would have to catch every day. In San Francisco, I only had the opportunity to catch at the school once or twice a week. People there encouraged my application to this organization, which was developing a substantial trapeze venue. I figured this would be the next logical step. After a phone interview, I received a plane ticket to Miami and a colorful volume of propaganda welcoming me to *the club*.

An employee in this French-based organization is referred to as a GO, short for *gentle organizer*. In essence, his job is to keep the party going for the people who are on vacation. This would be great for an aging fraternity boy with nothing else on his mind but play. For me, it was different. We were expected, literally every time we were out of our quarters, to be onstage. The powers that be, under the majesty of the *chef du village* (chief of the village), mingled about to make sure that we were entertaining the folks, from breakfast into late at night at the disco.

Again, I migrated to Florida in pursuit of my circus dream. The team greeted me after I got off the shuttle to The Sandpiper, the compound located in Port St. Lucie. Sarah and Jose, who were also there as associates of the pseudo circus, seemed nice enough. So did Jerry, the *chief of circus*. Yes, this was an actual title. Later, we made the connection that I had worked at Jerry's audition for Clown College in Denver about a decade earlier. Jerry was a seasoned veteran of the resort's circus arm, and eventually became a close friend. If there was anybody who could relate to my trapeze dream, it was Jerry. After Clown College, he had knocked around with a family mudshow for a while. I would later work as a clown for another member of the same family in Lima, Peru. Jerry had suffered severe hip and foot injuries through crash landings in performance. Now in his forties, he was still eager to fly. Jerry would need to train a catcher, and that would be me.

I did get to catch daily but never really adapted to the focus of this tourist-oriented circus training. The goal was to present two weekly shows. One was a display of circus skills, and the other, flying trapeze. Children got elementary instruction in acrobatics, trampoline, and physical comedy. One feature was the *Lions and Tigers* act, in which the "trainer" coached these "cats" (children on vacation) to jump through hoops and roll over. For me, doing my part in such acts was a means to an end. I reasoned that they were the dues I'd have to pay to become a catcher in a troupe. Pushing thirty, this ambition appeared to be a pipe dream. Still, I knew I had to try.

Both children and adults were invited to the afternoon trapeze classes. Circus GOs were expected to develop rudimentary flying skills and most of them enthusiastically did so. That didn't interest me. I was there to become a catcher.

I knew that in my late twenties, I was starting out too late to be a truly proficient flyer. What's more, it was always catching that attracted me. The desire to be on the flying end, though, was what seemed to entice most everyone else. My Uncle George, a former football coach, equated it to everybody wanting to be a halfback. The iconic song about the daring young man on the flying trapeze wasn't about the catcher. Still, I figured catching could become my way to latch onto a troupe. Interestingly, Gene Simmons from KISS related a similar strategy. Figuring the world was full of would-be rock guitarists, his ticket was to master the bass.

My living situation at the resort was tolerable enough, sort of like when I was living in the residence halls at San Francisco State. Another similarity was that I had a mission that most of those around me didn't have. Many college students are more preoccupied with partying than studying. In contrast, I was there to hit the books, so I got positive results. Most employees at the resort come for the festive atmosphere. Also, like dorm life in college, many of life's hassles are removed from the equation. No worries about traffic or lines at the grocery store. The concept was simple. We'd be fed, housed, clothed, and given a little money. The bottom line was to keep the guests entertained, morning into the night.

My own bottom line was to get to the next level as a catcher. In San Francisco, I had taken the #71 bus from my downtown apartment to the Haight-Ashbury neighborhood, where the trapeze stood in an old abandoned high school gym. At the Florida resort, however, the stainless-steel rig glistened in the sunlight. It was a three-minute stroll from where I slept. Outside of the occasional storm, characteristic of Florida's gulf coast, I could catch every day.

After their arrival, GOs were given a day to get acclimated. Jerry figured the rigors of this work would set in soon enough. However, I was ready to start catching right away. Jerry wanted to see my *catcher's lock,* so I climbed the thickly braided yellow nylon rope and got to work. Swinging rhythmically, I wrapped my legs around the cables in preparation for locking wrists with the flyer.

As he coached me on technique from the ground, I got a strong sense that I was in the right place, making the transition from being a novice to a professional catcher.

When it's right, catching people on the trapeze is like no other feeling in the world. I experienced brief instances of this utopia in the Florida resort, as Jerry let me catch him out of safety lines. This was when the magic happened. Jerry's trust in me grew as we worked together more and more. In the weekly trapeze show I was already catching vacationers. Nick, who had worked as a photographer for the club and caught members of the circus team in the performance, was scheduled to go on vacation. Jerry had me step in.

The catcher swings in controlled anticipation, and the world around him stops. He's now in charge. He makes sure to gauge the correct height of his swing to the trick that is being thrown to him. There's no time to second guess. Locked in, catcher and flyer instinctively recognize the appropriate takeoff time. Nevertheless, the catcher gives a "ready, hup," for proper timing. Gracefully going into his lock, the catcher takes comfort in the rhythmic creaking of the metal attachments. Both catcher and flyer feel the quiet tension of the release point. At this time the flyer was literally putting his life in my hands. If our effort was true, we'd grasp each other's wrists. However, the journey is only halfway completed. Our bodies must instantaneously work together and absorb the jolt of the return swing. A smooth, lithe flyer can make the return trip a joy. A timing mishap on either end can wrench the catcher's back or drop the flyer to go sliding down the apron of the net. Or worse.

I yearned to condition my mind and body to the point where such a dance became automatic and pure between me and the flyers. Since I had been a young child, I had watched these quietly powerful men make it look easy, snatching brave young acrobats from the jaws of disaster.

At the resort, the fact that I had spent two years with Ringling didn't seem to help me, and possibly was even somewhat of a hindrance. There were those who seemed to feel threatened because

I had actually been in a real circus. What's more, Canada's Cirque du Soleil was now in full bloom, and the glory days of Ringling had passed.

I began adapting to the rhythm of this lifestyle. Good food, a fun atmosphere, plus, thanks to Jerry, I was now working toward my goal as becoming a troupe-level catcher. Still, most of my catching was basic tricks from vacationers who were recreationally dabbling. However, I didn't complain. I figured that this served as a batting practice of sorts, building my speed and stamina. Bigger tricks, I figured, would come later.

We implemented strict safety procedures for the vacationers. One GO would be on the ground, minding the safety lines. Another was on the trapeze pedestal, supervising the belted novice. The pedestal attendant would release the individual holding the bar, and he or she would be essentially flying on the trapeze. The rhythm eventually became that of an amusement park ride, as vacationers would take turns for an hour.

The second hour, the one I lived for, was devoted to catching. I'd don my tights, climb up the heavy braided rope, and sit on my perch. Now I was in charge, calling the timing to synchronize the flyer to the specific trick that I was catching. If things worked out from both ends, the two parties would grab wrists in an intimate dance of timing and finesse. Two or three times, I jauntily replayed the scene from the movie *Trapeze* where Burt Lancaster catches Gina Lollobrigida then pulls her up and gives her a kiss. That was fun.

But the purest joy came when safety lines were removed. That's when the stakes got higher. The training wheels were off. It was a rise to the next tier, a significant step toward my becoming the catcher for *The Flying* _____.

I developed my skills well enough and was transferred to the Huatulco village in Oaxaca, Mexico. Villages from this organization provide a safe, somewhat antiseptic experience for visitors. There's the possibility for excursions outside of the compound, but many never leave during their stay. I was in southern Mexico, but I wasn't. A future as an aging cabaña boy wasn't for me. Like before, little else mattered to me than reaching the professional level as a catcher. My time in the Florida resort allowed me to catch with confidence out of safety lines. I anticipated that my experience in Huatulco would take me to the next step, so I took the dream with me to Mexico.

And how I did dream. Countless times as a spectator I watched the flyers stroll into the tent or arena in their capes and clogs. They remove and stylishly twirl their capes, then pass them to the ring attendant. The flyers and catcher go their separate ways. The flyers climb the ladder to their place on the trapeze pedestal. The catcher, with both hands, grabs the lip of the net and rolls onto it. He walks carefully and climbs, letting his body form a capital L. He straightens his legs and points his toes, demonstrating his strength while hand over hand, making his way to the catch bar. He chalks his hands and goes to work. If all goes right, the flyers are caught and returned to the pedestal gracefully. The catcher is traditionally the first one down, with a backward somersault into the net. He strolls to the edge and rolls out of it, back into his clogs. His job now completed, the catcher motions with his right hand to the pedestal for the flyers' dismounts. While I was on the way to my second resort village, I felt that I was closer to making that vision a reality. I figured that Huatulco would be the next step in my training.

It wasn't to be. My new circus chief designated himself the lead catcher. In Huatulco there were next to no adept flyers to catch anyway. The closest thing to a professional trapeze artist was his girlfriend, and she wasn't really interested in my catching her. My interest in working the pedestal and pulling safety lines waned, but I still looked forward to catching resort guests in the afternoon. My skills weren't growing.

My tenure at Huatulco started well enough. The resort was inhabited for a week by a group from Atlantis, a gay-friendly vacation company. The chief of circus had made it clear that he didn't want to catch homosexuals, so I was put through my paces early on. However, after that it wasn't in my supervisor's interest to train me to catch at the next level. He wanted somebody to mind vacationers on the pedestal and safety lines, making less work for himself. As I pushed thirty, it seemed that I was running out of time. If I was ever going to reach that next level, I had to do it *now*. My intensity on reaching that goal was an asset at the Sandpiper, but a hindrance in Huatulco. Jerry had sensed my passion about becoming a catcher and wanted to help me reach the next level. However, my new boss didn't care.

The circus chief in Huatulco also put the kibosh on my only time to shine in performance. I briefly shared a comedy routine with my buddy Paul Langas, the emcee for the village who was made for the job. Paul, close to seven feet tall and weighing around 300 pounds, was a natural for physical comedy. As I wrapped up my catching duties for vacationers who performed their trapeze tricks in front of the audience, Paul climbed the ladder of the rigging dressed as a woman. The spectators roared with laughter as Paul proclaimed that as my mother he carried me for nine months, and that the least I could do was catch him. Paul would grab the trapeze bar and leap from the pedestal while I would pretend to miss the catch and pull off his skirt, revealing brightly colored women's bloomers. The boss, seeing I was getting some attention, abruptly cut the gag from the performance.

The company had an absurd policy in its human resource practices. If a staff member decided that this type of life wasn't for him, he paid for his own plane ticket home. Such was the price for quitting. However, if he got fired, from wherever he was in the world, the company would spring for a one-way ticket back. Gilligan would return to civilization. It reached the point where I didn't care, one way or another. The beginning of the end for me was when my buddy Chris and I were lip-synching in yet another insipid stage show that we were required to perform. Chris dared me, and I grabbed a faux electric guitar, constructed of plywood, smashed it on the floor like Pete Townshend and walked off stage.

Not long thereafter, the circus chief blew a fuse. Making no bones about it, he declared, "You're a God *&%$, stupid *@#&ing idiot." Soon I was out of there. My friend Chris was similarly fed up with the place and also got himself released from service. We delayed our flights home a week, feeling we owed ourselves a vacation. The office cashed us out in pesos, with an exchange rate of about seven to a dollar. The large stack of foreign currency in my hand gave me the feeling of newfound freedom. A week in Puerto Escondido was just the ticket after months of restriction in the recreational compound. Long, balmy days, with miles of beach at our disposal. We had more than enough money for a cheap cabaña, food, and beer. Hospitable natives, at a moderate price, served steaming plates of whole-body prawns, right on the beach.

It was a perfect week, save one mishap. Our buddy Donald, who was still working at the village, met up with us on a day off. As a beginning surfer, he decided to catch the waves. Puerto Escondido is a world-renowned surfing spot, reserved for experts. Donald found out the hard way. Promptly, a crashing breaker slammed the board against his face. Donald was shaken up and endured some scrapes, nothing more. Still, it put a damper on our respite.

I arrived home, and it was time to get serious about life. Mom was still commuting to San Francisco, and I drove in with her to look for work. Within a week I got hired at Starbucks. It was the mid-nineties, and locations were sprouting like crabgrass. It was entirely possible to eke out a living this way in the city, where a car wasn't necessary. I got lucky. The same building where I had lived before, on the corner of Bush and Mason, had a vacant studio across the hallway from my old apartment. My Starbucks in the Financial District was a brisk walk from there. I returned to catching on the trapeze at the circus school. In some ways, it felt as though I had never left. But I had, and through my adventure and misadventure I realized that it was time to build a more solid career foundation. The idea of being an artist still appealed to me but not a starving one. I completed the mountain of paperwork required for substitute teaching and a second mountain to apply for a teaching credential. I chose San Francisco State, where I had previously spent four years as a dreamy undergrad. This time it was about putting myself on a direct career path. Still, occasion afforded me the chance to stroll through campus, wistfully reflecting on those joyful, reckless days and nights from years before.

While working toward my bachelor's degree, I had spent three years living in the residence halls. Campus housing had expanded since then, but during my stay there were three buildings for students, Mary Ward Hall, Mary Park Hall, and Verducci Hall. The first two were older six story structures, painted in earth tones. The newer building, the high-rise on campus, was Verducci. The fifteen-story white structure overlooked the campus with a sort of grandeur over an otherwise drab facility. If the buildings could talk, they would whisper, "You came here to study. That's it. You didn't pay a lot of money, so I won't afford you much luxury. The food, whether on a meal plan or bought in the student union, will be edible and filling. Come here, do your learning, and get out." It was a far cry from the stateliness of Stockton's University of the Pacific, where I would stroll just to take in the scenery.

I couldn't help but have a sense of nostalgia as I walked the campus again. College as an undergrad was fun. Now it was simply a facility where I was completing my certification. While I was studying for my credential, Verducci Hall had been declared a massive white elephant and was scheduled for demolition. Had it meant enough to me, I would have gone to the campus to witness the implosion. Strangely, one afternoon I saw the pile of broken concrete and plaster, which was once the building where I had slept for three semesters. It symbolized that I was letting go of some of my dreams.

Still, I managed to keep one or two wild ambitions in my pocket while involved in more pragmatic pursuits. I served as a substitute teacher five days a week and attended credential courses on evenings and Saturdays. I was putting some money away and planning for my future at my own pace. It seemed the right thing to do. I would eventually get where I was going, without winding myself into debt. That sense of self-determination had become a part of me, way back when I had gotten onto that Greyhound bus at seventeen to join Carson & Barnes. For better or worse, the circus had made my life more interesting. Little did I know there was more to come.

22. REBUILD

When I caught at the circus school I felt like a session musician. Showing up for the gig nonchalantly, climbing up the rope, playing my part, then going home. Trapeze was tucked comfortably into a corner of my life. I was also beginning to see the fruits of my post-resort career drive. I continued slinging lattes, while substitute teaching with success. Eventually the latter became a regular gig, and I was able to bid farewell to the Frappuccinos. I learned to adapt well to the clean-cut aspect of substitute teaching. I would go in, do what I was told, and leave at 3 PM. The next day I would be at the same school or somewhere else. It didn't matter. There were no office politics. No strings. Making a living this way probably wouldn't suit more sociable folks, but for me it worked fine.

I had freed myself from the resort cult (or it had freed itself from me) and was now reveling in life as a bachelor in San Francisco. Mild weather and an extensive (if not efficient) public transit system afforded me the opportunity to hop around town, working and playing to my heart's content. A sense of satisfaction that I hadn't experienced since my undergrad days at San Francisco State was coming back. I had missed the sense of building my own destiny that I had in college, busting my hump and getting good grades. Plus, I was able to put on my tights and climb up the rope to catch people, which I loved dearly. After we had gone our separate ways from the Sandpiper in Florida, Jerry had left the club around the same time as me. He turned up at the circus school one evening, and it was somewhat like old times.

After a while, my catching opportunity at San Francisco School for Circus Arts ended. That was followed by an unrewarding experience, somewhat similar to the resort at a summer camp in Pennsylvania's Pocono Mountains. I stopped catching and figured I had tucked away this activity forever. An adequate memoir could end here. A boy exits his adolescence in a highly unusual way, going on the road until he's twenty. On a whim, close to a decade later, he tries to come back to the circus as a performer and fails. Regrouping, his trapeze hobby leads to a resort job, and he nurtures for a while the remote possibility of catching in a troupe. But eventually there would be more.

Life hit hard at this time. My mother became ill and fought valiantly. She ultimately wouldn't recover. There are no words to describe the devastation. Somehow, I had to regroup. As it happened, part of my healing would come from catching again.

Three years had passed since I had climbed the rope to perch on my swing. I had heard that my old friends from San Francisco's trapeze school, Stephan and Lili Gaudreau, were opening their own rig. Stephan had been employed as a chef at the resort company and learned to fly on the trapeze there. He eventually mastered the art and performed the triple somersault at Circus Circus in Reno.

The plan was for the Gaudreau's new organization, *Trapeze Arts,* to inhabit an old warehouse in West Oakland. I felt as if I hadn't yet accomplished all I set out to do on the trapeze. As they say, if you love something, let it go. If it's meant to be, it will come back. It was time for the trapeze to come swinging back to me.

The interim facility was a middle school, closed for the summer. Rigging always baffled me, much to the frustration of my colleagues. This time it was ingeniously set up between two classroom buildings. Old friends began to pop up. I conditioned my body again for this kind of strain. My lower back protested the burden after the hiatus, but soon the aches faded and once again I was experiencing the sheer joy of this endeavor.

My work situation allowed me to devote substantial time that summer to trapeze. By then I had finished my first year of teaching sixth grade. A private school had hired me before the completion of my credential, and I signed on for a second year. With time on my hands, I borrowed a navy-blue station wagon from a friend and made the trek to the middle school in Walnut Creek, a half hour away. I was beginning my second act on trapeze, which coincided the development of a new company.

The gym opened that fall, and it was nice to be a part of the organization. We had our first meeting at Trapeze Arts, where I became a part-time employee. My friend Jerry came aboard, too. We took pride in the school, and the business was growing. Our maroon polos bore the whimsical Trapeze Arts logo. *STAFF* was emblazoned on my shirt, indicating that I was there with some measure of authority.

I returned to my teaching job, with limited hours for trapeze. Still, I used my time wisely, and my catching skills grew. Eventually I was entrusted to catch the advanced class on Friday nights, and I was called in for Saturday and Sunday classes as well.

My teaching career had reached a plateau. I had a successful second year in the private school, finishing my credential along the way. However, a public school experience the following year in San Francisco's East Bay proved dissatisfying.

I decided to go back to substitute teaching that fall. My life became wrapped up in trapeze like never before. I wanted to take this pursuit as far as it was meant to go.

I embarked on my marketing campaign. I placed an ad in *The Circus Report*, which was the standard trade publication for this business. There were no fancy graphics, just bold letters: TRAPEZE CATCHER. AVAILABLE NOW! I included my name and phone number, then the waiting began. I bought a SONY 8-millimeter video camera at The Good Guys and started obtaining footage of my catches from helpful observers on the ground.

Reaching for my dream, while minding the safety net. I had a teaching career that would wait. Trapeze wouldn't.

23. BONDS

I was living in my studio apartment, still dreaming my circus dream, substitute teaching to pay my bills. Bulking up on chocolate-flavored whey protein in a plastic jar from General Nutrition Center, along with weights at the San Francisco Embarcadero YMCA. Riding my bike to the Montgomery Street BART station and taking the train to catch recreational trapeze flyers in Oakland. Maybe I got to hold onto my dreams longer than most. Or maybe others' dreams in the backend of their thirties became more adultlike and included a steady job, marriage, and buying a house.

On occasion, I'd hitch a ride with a fellow trapeze enthusiast to Sam Keen's ranch in Sonoma. A bestselling author, Sam took up trapeze in his late fifties. He wrote his own book on this experience, *Learning to Fly*. Sam graciously welcomed me to his rig, nestled in the woods. I met Tony Steele there, the first man to complete the three and a half somersault. James Bond fans will note that Tony, in the opening scene of *Goldfinger,* splashes into a Miami pool after executing a triple somersault from the diving board. The legendary artist gave me invaluable guidance from the perspective of a flyer. Tony told me about a trapeze rig in Placerville, north of Sacramento, run by Christy Power. Christy had started out on the trapeze as a student at Florida State and eventually built a rig in her backyard. Trapeze people tend to find each other, and a catcher is always in demand.

In his time, Tony Steele was one of the world's greatest flyers, and I was delighted to catch him. Word got out that I was training to "go pro," as another catcher Hans put it. Graciously, he and others there gave me more time on the swing. They could see that I was a man on a mission.

The Sonoma rig became a critical part of my development as a catcher; it was where I first looked at the double somersault. In addition to Tony, a wild man named Dave was throwing it. The first time I hung for his double, Dave audibly snorted and strained on his backswing to obtain enough height, as I literally hung in there. I imagine a matador waiting with his cape shares similar feelings. Timing wasn't even close, and he accidentally kicked me in the face. I drove home with Jerry that afternoon with a black eye but didn't mind.

I sensed that I was making a breakthrough. Over a series of attempts, my brain would adjust to this endeavor. Soon, I was seeing the motion of the flyer more clearly as he tucked and rotated his body. Instead of a blur, the movement seemed to slow down. It appeared that I was now watching a film, frame by frame.

I returned to Sonoma, and Tony patiently kept throwing me doubles. Eventually, we grabbed each other's wrists. He shouted, "Are you happy now?" I was.

Chirpy banter on the rig was a mainstay during these times, belying the dangerous nature of this activity. The chitchat served to break tension for flyers, as they prepared to contort and hurl their bodies. Also, it's essential for the catcher and flyer to discuss adjustments to be made as they practice.

Tony is slightly hearing impaired, and sometimes we had trouble communicating with him on the rig. He joked about it. Playing a senile old man from a vaudeville riff, he'd repeat back, "Oh, you knew mother," when I made a completely unrelated remark.

In addition to my return to substitute teaching in San Francisco, I was working at Powell Place, a downtown time-share facility. The job was mostly sitting behind a desk, checking people into their hotel rooms. I'm a morning person, and the late hours threw my equilibrium off, especially the Thursday night graveyard shift, but I survived.

I used my catching aspiration as an excuse to connect with some of my longtime idols. I thought it would be a good idea to pick their brains. I called Bob Yerkes, who was considered the preeminent trapeze catcher of his day. I had seen him on *Circus of the Stars* years before, training sitcom actors to perform respectable trapeze maneuvers. After hearing what I was up to, Mr. Yerkes showed a great deal of encouragement. Elvin Bale and I also chatted on the phone. He was Ringling's daredevil for years. I remember Duane, the old clown, had a black and white snapshot of Bale posted inside the lid of his trunk in Clown Alley. As a child I saw him perform on the Wheel of Death when my Uncle George took me to the show at the Forum in Inglewood. In 1987, Bale flew past his landing after being shot from a cannon, and his fall caused paralysis to both legs. He was now in the business end of the circus.

I was resourceful in developing my network and began making vital connections. Once more, my circus dream would take me to Florida. A Cuban flyer named Alexis called me from Miami. In broken English he explained that he was looking for a catcher, and that was all the information I needed. The typical protocol would be for the leader of a troupe to send a plane ticket, along with agreeable terms for employment. However, at this point I was still untested, and I'd have to pay my own fare.

I was lucky and found us a rig to train on. A trapeze-oriented website led me to a guy named Frank Kora, who was running a rig in Boca Raton, forty-eight miles from Miami. He understood my dream. Frank had a background as a Ringling clown before becoming a trapeze artist. Our shared interest nurtured a fast friendship. We also discussed trapeze history, including its dark side. One late morning, we were lounging in Frank's suburban home, grounded from the rig because of rain. He showed me an issue of *Life* magazine from 1937, with an article on the Alfredo Codona tragedy. Codona, who was the preeminent flyer of his day, was forced into retirement because of an injury in 1934. During divorce proceedings in a Long Beach, California, attorney's office, Codona had shot and killed his third wife, Vera Bruce. Then he had turned the gun on himself.

Alexis and his welcoming mother lived in a small house in a low-rent section of Miami. They let me have the fold-out couch, and I tried to stay out of the way. Frank was all too pleased to give

142

us full access to the rig. I caught as I never had before. Like a climber taking a snapshot to prove he scaled Everest, I made sure someone was holding my video camera to capture the double somersault Alexis threw to me. Another Cuban named Poncho was a decent flyer, and we eventually completed the passing leap. As catcher, I'd wrap my arms around the knees of the first flyer (Poncho), while the second flyer (Alexis) balanced his body on top of the trapeze on the return swing. I'd fling Poncho back to the bar, he'd grab it, and Alexis would hurl himself over the bar, make a forward somersault (a maneuver called the forward over) then reach for me. I was now catching at the professional level. Alexis had hand-me-down trapeze costumes, white with purple sequins, and issued me one. Alexis and his mother smiled as I modeled it for them.

Frank helped me stay focused. After rehearsal one afternoon he told me on the phone that we were putting together "a nice little act." However, another catcher, a former resort guy, would pull up on his motorcycle and hang around the rig. His name eludes me, probably because I don't want to remember it. He had more experience and confidence, clearly a better catcher.

If there was a Robert Mitchum of trapeze catchers, it would be him. He had old straps from curtain rods, wrapping them around his wrists for grips. Like a telephone pole lineman climbing up to crimp a cable, he made no fuss, and didn't bother stretching. He didn't need tights; his street clothes worked just fine. I knew I was in trouble when he started catching Alexis. In the movie *Broadway Melody of 1940*, Eleanor Powell is in a casting agent's office, looking for a dance partner for her Broadway show. She takes one look at the hoofer (George Murphy), then nods and smiles approvingly at the agent. From the trapeze pedestal, Alexis gave Frank the same look. Nevertheless, with Frank's encouragement, I stuck around for a few more days. I called Lisa, my girlfriend at the time, to give her an update. That would include staying in Miami a while longer and quitting my job at the hotel. Lisa responded with, "I know you. You have stars in your eyes." However, she didn't quite get it. What

I really had, was the burning need to pursue this endeavor while I still could. I wasn't ready to walk away. Not yet.

Alexis, Poncho, the catcher, and a teenage girl who could fly some would eventually go on to the gig, and I flew home. I had no regrets. I had substitute teaching to come back to, as well as my catching at Trapeze Arts. I had made it to the next level as a catcher, though a berth in a troupe still eluded me. Frank and I, in one of our rigside chats, agreed that I was like a minor league ballplayer at the triple-A level, just a hair below major league qualification. Frank was encouraging, but I also knew I could rely on him to provide a realistic assessment.

It felt good to get home and pick up my life. I brought my tape to display at Trapeze Arts, and my buddies there were adequately impressed. I was welcomed back to the Oakland rig. However, the trade-off was that in my absence I had been replaced catching Friday night's advanced class. Nevertheless, I made my way back into catching whenever I got the chance and continued my marketing campaign. By now I had a standard package. I would prepare a brief cover letter and enclose a small head shot that had my name and phone number at the bottom. I enclosed catching footage, including the double somersault and passing leap. The contents went into a box designed for mailing a VHS tape. I'd then walk to the bottom of Nob Hill to send my kits from a branch post office in the basement of Macy's.

I didn't know how Carlos got my number. I didn't care. I got home one night, and he had left a message on my answering machine. I called him back. A thick Latino accent proclaimed he was putting together a show in Lima, Peru and wanted me to be a clown in it. It would be six week's work. I countered that I was training to catch on the trapeze, and Carlos said that he would arrange for a rig there where I could work out. Later, he had told me that as a youngster he had been a catcher in his family's troupe. Carlos would relate to me that on his thirteenth birthday, his father told him to "get his #@& up there," and so his career began. Interestingly, his line of interview questions included asking me if

144

I was gay, as a single man in his thirties, living in San Francisco.

Eventually, we established a good rapport during the phone chat and sealed the deal. But it was *only* a possibility at this point. By now, I had been at this game long enough to realize that these things tend to fall through more often than not. My dad was amused upon my announcement that I might be going to Peru. I went on with my routine. After I received the plane ticket in the mail, I told myself that this was really happening.

I pieced together clown costumes from days past and bought some greasepaint. Deanna, a friend of my sister's, is an expert milliner, so I had her make me a little white felt hat, for a European look. I also packed some tights because I would be doing some catching there. I still had my passport from the resort days in Mexico. Timing was perfect. I'd leave in July and come back in August, in time to resume my substitute teaching.

When I arrived in the Lima airport, I knew that I was truly in foreign territory. Jetlagged, I gathered my luggage and gazed at strangers approaching me. It took a while for it to register that they were industrious *taxistas* trolling for fares. I managed to exchange currency, picking at the unfamiliar-looking coins in my palm. I found a bright blue payphone from Telefonica, a Spanish company, to give Carlos a call. He'd send someone to pick me up.

A while later, a young couple arrived. They could have just as well been a yuppie pair from the states. The woman would start out as our ringmastress but after a couple days would be the first casualty of a bloodletting while Carlos tried to keep his show afloat. The typical warmth I experienced with Peruvians was exemplified by my new chums. They considerately asked me if I was hungry, and so settled in for my first meal in Lima. We went to Norky's, a mainstay chain restaurant in the city that would eventually become a friend to return to in subsequent visits. We chomped *pollo a la brasa* (rotisserie chicken) with *papas fritas* (French fries) and became acquainted. They introduced me to *Inca Kola,* an industrial yellow-colored soda that tastes like bubble gum. This was the farthest I had ever travelled, but strangely it had the feeling of home.

24. AMAUTA

More than one individual had warned me about getting involved with this circus impresario's family. Indeed, I didn't hang
my financial well-being on this endeavor. I liked to keep flexibility
at this time in my life. Substitute teaching, along with odd jobs,
paid the rent and a little extra for savings. *Plan B* was well in place.
If the show went belly up and I ceased to get paid, which was, in
fact, what happened, I'd just go back to my little life in San
Francisco.

My only knowledge of the city of Lima was that it was the capital
of Peru. I learned this fact in Mr. Bratton's sixth grade class, in a
social studies unit on South America.

My new friends dropped me off at the assigned hotel and I col-
lapsed in bed. I got up the next morning for a quick jog. I was then
introduced to the eight Argentinian showgirls. I appreciated their
cultural tradition of kissing a new acquaintance on the cheek. One
was named Solange and resembled Gina Lollobrigida.

We piled into a van and were driven to the Coliseo Amauta. I
was enthralled to return to the enticing familiarity of a performance
venue ready to spring into action. In a far corner, tigers nervously
paced back and forth in their small cages. Riggers above were doing
whatever it is they did. Carlos eventually showed up and greeted
me with a bear hug. His wife, some forty years younger, brought
him clear, liquid heart medicine in a plastic cup. Anthony Quinn
would have been the perfect actor to play Carlos. His first order of
business was asking to borrow my passport, to register me as an
employee. I respectfully declined, having been warned back home
to never surrender this document. I didn't wish to insult my new
boss, but I also sensed the need to protect myself. Carlos relented,
and we took a taxi to the American embassy across town. I didn't
think it was a good idea for Carlos to show up in a government
building sporting the gaudy curl of a three-inch lion claw hanging
from a chain around his neck. I kept this criticism to myself. He

had proudly announced that it was a gift from legendary animal trainer Wolfgang Holzmair. Carlos had a circus career as a performer and impresario that extended through Atlantic City, the World's Fair in New Orleans, and Ringling. Sadly, he was going out with a flicker instead of a bang.

The Coliseo Amauta had also seen better days. Its claim to fame was being the site of 1982's Miss Universe contest. Footage shows Bob Barker, in his typical courtly manner, coronating Miss Canada, Karen Baldwin. As millions worldwide tuned in, the statuesque Baldwin towered symbolically over a diminutive runner-up from Guam, Patty Chong Kerkos. But sadly, like so many buildings in Lima, I was to find, the venue now held unfulfilled promise. Two decades after the big pageant, I saw in her a sweet sadness. The paint of the building's interior was peeled, and the leaky roof was patched together. Dreariness was underscored by the damp, cool July weather, winter in that part of the world. The coastal climate prevented freezing in Lima, so there was no central heat in the facility. Or if heat was available, management didn't bother switching it on. The metal and concrete structure seemed to hold in the cold as opposed to provide shelter from it. There were scant crowds, and the cast was whittled to a skeleton crew. The Argentines left first, the showgirls and two teenage boys and a girl who had a trampoline act. It was quiet behind the curtain and in the hotel after that; they had been a jovial group. Carlos decided to get rid of me, too, but I talked him into letting me stick around. I was having fun in Lima and had a place to stay.

My average hotel room, compared to my sweat box at Carson & Barnes and the roomette at Ringling, was palatial. Unlike a typical stop during a circus season, we were in Lima for more than a month. The city began to get a familiar feel.

More than this, while I was there, fate had intervened, and my life was changed. At the show, we worked hard on weekends, three performances per day. The rest of the week, we performed just one show at night, which gave me opportunity to knock around the city. Downtown, I recognized the Sheraton hotel.

The basement of the Sheraton houses a small shopping concourse. Tourists can pick up Peruvian artwork, alpaca garments, and handicrafts for seriously inflated prices, without leaving the comfort of the hotel.

I sauntered through the door of the gift shop, and she smiled at me. It took her a while, but I fell at first sight. She told me her name, Cecy, short for Celia. Life in Lima during these weeks took a light, breezy pace, and I would drop by the Sheraton to visit my new friend.

I treasured the familiarity of getting to the arena early. The nearly empty building, like those in the states, had a way of echoing while I had a conversation with somebody. I enjoyed jogging along the upper deck of the circular arena. I'd almost put myself in a trance, trotting along in a clockwise motion, with the feeling of no beginning and no end.

After Carlos and I had *the talk*, establishing that I was merely earning a bed, there was a tremendous sense of freedom. I figured that I wasn't getting paid to be there, so I might as well enjoy myself. The other clown in the show was a talented Ecuadorian who went by *Chicho*. It was easy to see why Carlos really didn't need me there. Chicho wowed the audience and pulled spectators from the crowd to participate. He brilliantly dressed his small dog in an elephant costume and trained him to march along the ring curb and follow his commands. Chicho's auguste make-up fit his bubbly personality. His costumes were elegant satin affairs with top hats and tails, in vibrant colors. When he graciously included me in gags we developed, I was happy to be the one to take the falls, in my washable cotton clown garb. Chicho eventually became the ringmaster, too, announcing acts from behind the curtain.

After the performance, I'd sometimes grab a taxi and go across town to the San Miguel section of Lima, where I'd practice catching flyers from another show. The group welcomed me

148

warmly, and the small circus tent took me back to Carson and Barnes, twenty years prior. I befriended Calin Coronel, who ran the show. I would go to work in his circus as a clown the following June. In short order, I carved out a place for myself in Lima's circus community, treasuring my time there. I was still paying rent on my studio apartment back in San Francisco, though, knowing that I'd soon return to my relatively conventional life. Still, I wanted to enjoy Lima while I could. I had saved enough money to be there a while, and as always, my time in that city was sweet.

There was no cookhouse or pie car, but I managed to stay well fed on my tight budget. In the morning, I'd flip through the pages of *El Comercio,* Lima's newspaper, in the lobby while partaking of the so-called continental breakfast at Hotel Bypass, consisting of stale bread and watery coffee. The dollar was strong compared to the sol, Peru's currency, so I had no trouble affording food. I managed to find staples, such as miniature *plátanos* (bananas) and liquid yogurt, at a small *mercado* (grocery store) close to the arena. Upon occasion I'd sample other delicacies along the way, such as the fried coconut pieces sold by a vendor. I found a little café close to the building and sometimes treated myself to a delightful pre-show meal of *lomo saltado.* I grew to love this traditional Peruvian dish of sliced beef, potatoes, and vegetables. I became friends with the lady who ran the establishment, as well as her eleven-year-old daughter, who was learning English. I was pleasantly surprised when I saw them at a performance while I was greeting the audience. I also enjoyed *emoliantes,* jojoba and fruit juice concoctions, served hot from stands on street corners. Like an old friend, the tinkling of the vendor's stirring spoon on glass in the open air comes back to greet me when I visit Lima. I didn't know the ingredients in the greenish brown liquid and didn't want to. On a long exploratory walk one afternoon, I stopped at another roadside stand and treated myself to ceviche, raw fish cooked in lime juice that Peru is famous for. Later, I was informed that buying this delicacy along the pavement was an unsafe practice.

I never became ill from my varied food experimentation in Lima, so it was indeed ironic that I got sick on my last day there, after Cecy and I ate at a seemingly innocuous Chinese restaurant. Throughout Lima there are scores of inexpensive, generic restaurants selling *chaufa*. Chaufa is Peru's version of Chinese food, with variations of rice, noodles, meat, vegetables, and scrambled eggs piled high.

Gratefully, Cecy was fine after our meal. I wasn't. After lunch, I went back to the hotel to pack. I rarely get sick but instantly knew I was in trouble. My gut felt like it had been worked over by a claw hammer. That evening I managed to get to the airport and drag myself to the Continental Airlines counter. I propped myself up and struggled to produce my ticket and passport. I could tell that the airline officials were questioning whether they should let me get on the plane. Someone who spoke English was summoned. Fortunately, I was able to convince him to let me through the ticket counter, and then they placed me in a wheelchair. If you're ever flying internationally and want to get through immigration quickly, just tell them you're sick with food poisoning. I was immediately taken to the front of the line.

Mercifully, a flight attendant let me lie down in some vacant seats on the plane. I rested in relative comfort on the long trip back to the states and then had a connecting flight from Houston. I felt much better by the time I got on the second plane. Still, I was pale and all around unhealthy looking. My coach seat back to San Francisco was between two attractive young ladies. However, looking like a cadaver and smelling of sweat and vomit, I figured it best not to flirt with them.

My life resumed after my trip to Lima. Timing was good, as a new school year was starting, and I was again able to substitute teach. Even better, I was hired by a school as the site support substitute. This meant that I would stay at the same school each day, without the hassle of finding day-to-day sub work. Plus, I didn't have to be concerned with developing lesson plans or correcting papers. I even received medical benefits. Life slipped into a routine, and I continued catching people on the Oakland trapeze during weekends. Along the way, Cecy and I kept in touch online. She invited me to her sister's wedding, which would take place that December. The next family wedding would be ours.

But for now, I was to retool my catching efforts, as the circus dream was appearing as a last vestige. I had left Ringling at twenty and didn't return to being a circus clown until the age of thirty-seven. I would give trapeze one last shot.

I had seen individuals who had completely devoted their careers to the circus, only to become embittered in the end, with nowhere else to go. I never wanted to feel that way about an art form I loved so dearly. That's one reason why I hit the books and worked diligently on more conventional career endeavors *on the outside*. It was a wise choice. After my time as a Ringling clown, I would become involved with the circus again, as a performer, writer, or mere spectator. Still, I wanted it to remain a beloved, magical world. I had to establish a life outside of the circus so I could gain a greater appreciation of life inside of it.

In contrast, Carlos, like many circus people I had met, was born into that life. He never knew anything else. As it turned out, the show at Coliseo Amauta would be Carlos' swan song, the last show he'd produce. On a later trip to Lima, I called him on the phone. He was now living in Guayaquil, Ecuador. Carlos was elated to hear about my new married life. That was the last time I talked to him. Sometime later, I found out he had died.

25. PAHRUMP

Alexis called. Again. If New York's Madison Square Garden was the highlight of my life in the circus, a municipal park in Pahrump, Nevada, would decidedly be the low. Alexis, who had replaced me in Miami, asked me to catch for him. By then, I was thirty-eight. Realistically, it was my last chance. Perhaps, it was a ridiculous notion to think that this endeavor could be successful, but I decided to give it a shot.

An *act* can take months to prepare; we had a few days. This truly wasn't the best of circumstances, but I was aware that at my age, this would probably be my last chance to catch on a trapeze in the circus. Meanwhile, Alexis, though not entirely proficient in his second language of English, managed to express adequately my shortcomings as both a rigger and catcher. I decided to stick it out and endure his barbs, vowing to improve myself.

Our *troupe,* such as it was, had the name of the *Flying Trasancos.* Apparently, it was some sort of a family name for Alexis. A theatrical agent let us set up the trapeze rigging on a patch of dirt behind his small office building, a few miles from the Strip. Alexis was miffed with me for being less than proficient in assembling the rig. We finally hauled it up and it felt good to sit on the swing. From my perch, I could make out the Y-shaped pattern of Mandalay Bay. My previous Vegas trip was for a wedding there, a couple who had flown at Trapeze Arts in Oakland.

We practiced with dubious results. The catcher and flyer, when aligned, flow together in a graceful dance. When it's right, they become as one. Alexis and I never quite achieved this chemistry. The second flyer's name eludes me. I *do* remember that he spoke essentially no English, and what's more, had never previously been on a flying trapeze.

The physical and emotional stress took their toll, as I was truly depleted by day's end. Sleep came without a problem, whether it was on the floor of Alexis' buddy Danny's apartment in Vegas, or my designated section in the stuffy second or third-hand RV Alexis bought for the gig. Danny was performing his own aerial act at the Rio hotel and was a most gracious host.

Alexis broke out old video cassettes at Danny's place. Every flyer seems to have a stash of home movies. Proudly, he pointed out his deftness in the air. Nameless shows had featured him as a flyer. Footage also showed Alexis training under modest circumstances, on a rig fastened to rickety buildings in a rundown section of Havana. He pointed out the flawless technique of his former catchers. Alexis was trying to encourage me, but it was having the opposite effect. My self-confidence waned.

Pahrump is a long hour's drive from Las Vegas. Talk radio fans may recognize this town's name as the location where Art Bell would broadcast his show. We were to join up with a tiny circus run by the Osorio family. More than two decades prior, in Carson & Barnes, this family featured their three sons and daughter on the high wire. The ringmaster, Robert, had only been ten back then but still remembered me.

My lack of rigging prowess continued to be an issue when we set up in Pahrump. However, for the first time, I was setting up the trapeze for *me* to catch on it in the circus. I was determined to do it better, diligently taking notes on a pad along the way. I figured there was no way around it. Learning to set up the rigging adequately was a part of the job, a skill I would have to acquire. Alexis went through his usual grumblings, and again we managed to haul up the rig. Now I would climb to *my* perch, feeling I truly belonged there for the first time. I sat on the swing a while, thinking about how far I'd come. Perhaps I thought too much about what was happening, instead of letting this potentially splendid event merely take its course.

A matinee and evening performance were scheduled. I'd catch Alexis on a layout, a somersault without a tuck. This was the first trick Jerry threw to me out of safety lines at the resort. I would then catch the rookie flyer's knee hang, the most basic of tricks on the trapeze. Finally, we would attempt the double somersault.

Our entire act consisted of three catches, pretty much impossible to forget. Nevertheless, I wrote the sequence on my right wristband as a reminder. The flyers thought this was funny.

I knew the drill from a scene with Tony Curtis in the movie *Trapeze*. He had wrapped a robe around himself over his costume to check the rigging. I wore a warmup suit over my costume, red with yellow, sequined flames. But it wasn't really mine, and the Lycra was too tight. Alexis told me he had inherited this set of costumes from a friend. I could have watched the show before our act, but I didn't. Recorded music accompanied the acts. Somebody used Ricky Martin's *Livin' La Vida Loca*.

By the time it was our turn to go on, I felt ready to jump out of my skin. I excitedly proclaimed to Alexis that this was a dream come true. He remained silent and stoic, which I should have also done. Robert announced us, and I climbed to my perch. Getting into the lock, hanging upside down to catch the flyer, would be rote. The layout would be routine, the knee hang, even easier. The one obstacle, which would or wouldn't justify my reason for being there, was whether Alexis and I would complete the double somersault. The act started off as expected. I began to feel a groove as Alexis and I executed the layout handily. The rookie's knee hang was no problem, either. We didn't come close to returning it to the pedestal, but Alexis didn't expect that from a beginning flyer. Next would be the double. I knew that I had to be aggressive, starting out by swinging at a high arc. Back in Sonoma, Tony Steele had told me that the catcher needs to swing with the cables on this trapeze at a *buckling* arc. Alexis caught his breath. I swung high into the warm night air and executed my lock. We missed. Alexis looked at me as if I had stolen money from him. On some level, maybe I did. The fact that our troupe was so hastily thrown together served as an ample excuse. Then again, perhaps I was out of my league, plain and simple. Robert kept his announcing upbeat, explaining that the wind was a factor. There was a slight breeze.

Try again. I hung upside down, knowing this could be the most important catch of my life. Or the most important miss. Our hands wrapped around each other's wrists, commanding every iota of my attention. Lost in the moment, my legs let go from their lock around my swing. In an instant I was pulled from the net, where my face and chest broke the fall. I think I knew in that moment the performance and gig were finished. In effect, my career as a circus trapeze catcher started and finished instantly. I rolled out of the net and held my hands up to the spectators, signaling I was okay. I wasn't. My forehead was bleeding, and there was a gash on my nose. *The Flying Trasancos* were the final act in the show, and on that afternoon, we truly provided a finale. The entire cast had come out for a bow. The young female performer standing next to me had a sympathetic smile. Some guy from the audience felt moved to walk up and shake my hand. The three of us in the shoddily formed troupe strolled back to the RV, and I pretty much knew it was over. Alexis managed a fairly eloquent speech. He proclaimed that he had a daughter, and as such, valued his life. This was a direct implication that my screw-up put his life in danger. He maintained that I was a good guy *and* a good catcher, but that this couldn't continue. Alexis mentioned that he'd pay for my flight home from Las Vegas. He would never get around to that. In addition, he said he'd talk to Mr. Osorio about keeping me on, possibly as a clown. I began pleading with Alexis that I still wanted to be his catcher, but didn't feel like fighting too hard. I knew it was time to let go, literally and figuratively. The discussion eventually cooled with the setting of the twilight sun. A warm May night in southern Nevada.

In the movie *Field of Dreams,* ghosts of baseball players come back to Earth to hit, throw, and catch again. One of those who appeared from the Iowa cornfield was *Moonlight Graham.* His major league career consisted of one appearance in right field, and no ball was hit his way. He never stepped up to bat. His character makes the choice to save the life of a little girl watching the game, who is choking. To do this, he had to step across the chalk base paths, never to return to the game he loved. Burt Lancaster, God rest his soul, plays Moonlight Graham's ghost, and saves the little girl's life. I hope Mr. Lancaster, the old circus acrobat, is up there smiling as this role he played is intertwined into a trapeze story.

In Hugo, Oklahoma, there is a cemetery dedicated to circus performers, *Showmen's Rest*. The facility features a monument with the following caption: A TRIBUTE TO ALL SHOWMEN UNDER GOD'S BIG TOP. I like to think there's a heaven... and that it has a trapeze. In it, my tireless soul will grasp the wrists of the awaiting flyers, with smooth precision every time. I also like to think that I'd respond with the same nobility if faced with a similar dilemma as Moonlight Graham's.

When my one-performance trapeze career ended, a sense of peace overtook me. I walked the half mile to a pay phone outside of a Walmart. It was time to let my sister know what had happened. I mentioned how, as an aging catcher, I didn't want to risk hurting a flyer as my skills declined. I thought it was profound to note that my writing, in contrast, presented no such hazards. Lynne quipped that the only danger could come from me boring my readers to death.

Jim Craig was the goalie for the U.S. Olympic hockey team in 1980, which won the gold medal. Thirty years later, he related that the Soviet players had looks of relief on their faces after being defeated. There's a sense of resolve when a climb ends, even when a summit isn't reached.

The evening of the crash, I figured I'd show enough class to help Alexis take down his rigging. Mercifully, this time he didn't belittle my lack of mechanical prowess. We took our time. By now the adrenaline had worn off, and soreness was setting in. That night I curled up in the RV, feeling as if someone had kicked me in the ribs. It was the net that had kicked me and saved my life at the same time. The next morning Alexis wasn't forthcoming about his plans. I talked him into dropping me off at a Las Vegas hospital. I figured I should get checked out. The kind, young doctor gave me a tetanus shot and X-ray. Nothing was broken. Physically, at least. He prescribed a generic form of Vicodin for the pain in my chest. I got a taxi to the airport and was on my way home. During the ride from the hospital, the friendly cabbie and I looked through the windshield and chatted about the temporary nature of hotels on the Strip. It seemed strange that these magnificent structures, Mandalay Bay, Bellagio, Luxor, could very well be imploded in the future, making way for something even bigger and better.

My sister and brother-in-law picked me up at the Oakland airport; I needed help with my luggage. I got home to San Francisco and recovered in my studio apartment. The prescribed narcotic and reflection on my experience produced a haziness in my brain. I stopped taking the prescription, still sore but not in excruciating pain. The drug started feeling good, and I didn't want to get used to it.

My professional *safety net,* substitute teaching, was in place. I landed squarely. Gratefully, this net provided a much softer landing than the one in Pahrump. I returned to my job and finished up the school year as a site support substitute teacher, which I loved. Upon my arrival a boy greeted me with a bear hug. I clutched my chest, wincing in pain.

I prepared for a new chapter in my life. I needed to return to Lima, sensing that my future was with Cecy. It was time to get more serious about my teaching career, which I did. For a while I continued to catch on the trapeze in the Oakland school as a hobby. My chest was sore as I mended from my fall. Still, I knew it was important to get back up there. I didn't want to be afraid of the trapeze, reasoning the importance of *getting back on the horse.* Dad had taught me that as a boy. While visiting Dad at his home in Modesto, he gave me an additional lesson, that I had to let go of the trapeze at the professional performance level. Dad had torn up his knees playing football at San Jose State and could relate well to how hard it can be to stop something he loved. He struggled to remain on the gridiron, playing semi-pro for a team in the beach town of Santa Cruz. Then Dad knew when to quit and strongly suggested the same for me. It was time.

Throughout some thirty years, at varying times and levels of intensity, I had dreamed of catching on the trapeze in the circus. In a split second, I reached farther than I could firmly and safely grasp, while a tiny audience at a park in Pahrump watched my failure. I now frequently remind myself, relieved, that the practice of writing is by contrast, intensely private. As you read this, you will never need to know of the process that led to ultimately bringing these typed words to the printed page. It comforts me that I don't have to show a reader the reams of scribblings and rewrites, which ultimately led to the final product. Gratefully, I can't fall from my notebook. Anne Frank shared in her journal, while hiding from the Nazis, that *paper is patient*.

The trapeze wasn't patient. I never caught the triple somersault, but I *did* catch the double and passing leap, if only in practice. For years to come, I can bore house guests with home movies of these feats, from a rig behind the YMCA in Boca Raton. Maybe I'll mention the boss chose another catcher, eventually went with me, and booted me after one performance. Maybe not. Gradually, through time, ink, and paper, I continue to work the flying trapeze out of my system. Dad, after my mishap, told me I was lucky I hadn't broken my neck. I remind myself to count my blessings. Paper is patient. It's also safe.

26. GRINGO

I finished the school year after my trapeze accident and then latched onto a circus produced by my buddy Calin, whom I met during my first trip to Lima. His family, the Coronels, put together a small show. June through August, numerous productions like this dot the city. The annual tradition had brought me there the previous July. These circuses often adopt gimmicks to entice audiences. Carlos' show at Coliseo Amauta had incorporated *Las Vegas* in its title, ironic in the setting of the crumbling arena. The Coronels' show had an African theme. There was a painted marquee of sorts on a white brick wall. The star of the show was nonhuman, a twenty-foot-tall, white gorilla doll, complete with pulleys to move its arms and mouth.

It's tradition to kick off such shows with a press conference, and Calin requested my presence. Even though he wasn't in the show, all seven feet five and eight-tenths inches of *Margarito* were also there. Peruvians all seemed to recognize him by his first name. While Margarito was nowhere near the height of the World's Tallest Man, he was Peru's Tallest Man, some sort of title. Margarito was a local celebrity in Lima, making a living from appearances of this type. After the press event, my experience with Coronel's show was largely uneventful.

It felt good to be working again in Lima, and it felt even better to get paid. It was easy to slip into a loosely based structure. The job would be only for a few weeks. Calin and I figured there wasn't any reason to bother with a work visa. A matinee and evening show occurred every day, though a schedule in Lima was no more than a general idea. The performance would start whenever Calin decided enough customers had shown up.

It seemed the climb was completed. Calin was elated to have a former Ringling clown working for him, and I could basically do whatever I wanted in the show. I was now the clown with tenure. San Miguel, this part of Lima, had become familiar. I'd usually be up by seven or eight, early by circus people's standards. The show was settled in one place, and it had a pleasant familiarity to it. I'd often go for a run to start my day, pleased that I was in a foreign land, earning my keep. In a way, San Miguel had the feeling of any American suburb. A short walk away from the hotel was a supermarket with the simple name of *Wong*, Peru's equivalent of Safeway. I rustled up my familiar rations, bananas, oranges, and bread, purchasing enough to get me through the day at the big top. From there it was a leisurely saunter to the tent, and I would put on my greasepaint.

Even though it was winter in Lima, the weather was mild. Behind the circus tent, a small-time entrepreneur set up an open-air diner. I'd bolt down some *arroz con pollo* (chicken with rice) between calls on the floor. For a few soles (around $1.50 in American currency exchange) I could fill my belly. I had the chance to acquire secondhand paperbacks in English during occasional excursions downtown, devouring them in the performers' tent during breaks in the show. I enjoyed the chance to socialize with my colleagues, a jovial bunch. At the end of the night's work, sometimes I'd share the ring and practice juggling while my pal Christopher polished his hand balancing act. Then I'd stroll home in the cool night wearing a warm-up suit, still in greasepaint. My digs were comfortable enough, a bare-walled hotel room, about a half mile's walk from the big top. The desk clerk, never impressed, would hand me my room key. I think he remained miffed after I complained once that the hot water ran out.

Reality back home would wait for a while. For now, life was simple in the circus. Calin didn't hassle me, but I made sure to show up early for work. I figured it was the least I could do. While cast and crew usually got along, a scuffle did break out in a recreational soccer game before a matinee. This also happened during my first trip to Lima. Peruvians take the game seriously. As a goalie, I was safely separated from the conflict both times.

Time passed merrily. With glee I'd meet and greet the audience, inside and outside of the tent. I treasured these times, knowing it could be my last experience performing in the circus.

The circus was winding down in San Miguel. Calin offered me the opportunity to stay with the show longer, playing somewhere in the Peruvian jungle. I declined. I was ready for a break, wanting time with Cecy before heading back to the states. Without fanfare, the show ended one night. My circus career was now quietly tucked away.

27. SINCE

In the summer of 2009, my wife Cecy and I had the opportunity to go back to visit the Carson & Barnes Circus. Calin, my buddy from Lima, emailed me that a couple I had worked with was over there. Small world. A highlight of my time during my final engagement under the big top in Peru was attending the christening of their baby in the ring. We made the forty-five-minute drive from Sacramento to Lodi and shared a delightful reunion. In addition to chatting with pals from a continent away, I talked with a clown who had been trying to hook up with Ringling. The circle continued.

A couple years later, Cecy and I went back to visit Calin's show. This time it was in Rimac, an outlying section of Lima. It was scaled down even smaller, with room under the big top for around a hundred spectators. Calin's brother Paco spotted me and acknowledged my presence through the tiger cage before performing his act. A cat got loose in the transportation process, and the animal was running for a while underneath the tent. One way or another, this weird, wonderful world moves forward.

In her masterful novel *Water for Elephants,* Sara Gruen's elderly central character, Jacob Jankowski, yearns to live out his final days with a traveling circus. Come to think of it, perhaps that wouldn't be a bad way to go. There are times when I think that I should stay away until then. I'm sure the sense of magic a seventeen-year-old feels for the circus can resurface, even six or seven decades later. As George Carlin proclaimed, "Old people are just bent kids." Then again, the circumstances may point to a return some time in between. Just in case, I hold onto my old steamer trunk. I like to think that before my life is over, I'll experience being on the road again with some show. I suppose if it's meant to be, it will. Meanwhile, I have my memories and my pen.

There's a sharp contrast between observing the circus as a spectator and writing a memoir about it. I still crane my neck while watching a performance. By design, the collage of color, movement, and sound is an overwhelming sensory experience. My pulse still races as I struggle to take it all in. I don't think this book could have been a truly effective one if I were still working for a show. I'd be reporting on events as they were happening, far different than thoughtful reflection on this unconventional way of life. I'm comforted by having hours to mull over my thoughts, as opposed to hundredths of a second to catch a double somersault.

The labor over a book doesn't give the immediate gratification experienced by a circus performer. Both the flyer and catcher know instantly if their endeavor has been a successful one. A clown immediately feels an audience's approval of his antics... or doesn't. And of course, a juggler knows if he worked his props well for the crowd. With words, I must wait.

Five years had passed since my ill-fated trapeze venture in Las Vegas, and my next trip to Vegas was for fun. Naturally, a personal highlight was Circus Circus. Alas, the facility had seen better days. Faded pink trim decorating the white buildings showed that nobody was bothering to renew the hotel, which had opened in 1968. Tony Steele was one of the trapeze flyers. Interestingly, that was also the year of the first Clown College class. In 1996, the seemingly immortal Sands was imploded, making way for the Venetian. The Stardust and Aladdin met the same fate. Is Circus Circus next? Hopefully, I'll again be able to duck into one of the purple plastic seats and see a finely muscled young man catch a triple somersault.

As I strode by the noisy slot machines to find the performance venue, I felt a pang of nostalgia for when I, myself, was pursuing a career in spandex and sequins. I made sure to be on time for the first show of the day. A thoroughly entertaining clown performed a barbecue gag with fire and a huge foam rubber steak. He was followed by a husband/wife acrobatic act. My eyes instinctively found the dangling catcher's trapeze, which would inevitably be used later. Waiting for the show to start, I reflected on how I lost my concentration and got pulled out of my swing, sixty-two miles east in Pahrump. That was far behind me, though, and I could enjoy the circus from a distance.

After the morning's performance, I asked the sleepy-eyed drummer about clowns from my old Ringling Brothers days, whom I heard were working for Circus Circus. Two of them were still there, and another pair had become lawyers. Feel free to insert an obvious joke of your own here.

I'm content to watch some other guy perched on his swing. There will always be *some other guy.* For anyone reading this, I beg you, *carpe diem,* seize the day. We never know how much time we have to pursue our hearts' desires.

Many leave circus life with wounded bodies and hearts. At the end of the movie *Trapeze,* Mike (Burt Lancaster) instructs a catcher on handling the flyer Tino (Tony Curtis) with his triple somersault. Mike says, "Now that he's got it, don't let him lose it." The troupe had just been hired to join Ringling Brothers, but Mike declines because of conflict over the woman in the act, Lola (Gina Lollobrigida). Mike, permanently injured from a previous trapeze injury, limps away at the end. A woman from his past, Rosa (Katy Jurado), runs to catch up with him, but we don't know what the future holds. There's a time to leave the circus. Mike Ribble and I sensed when it was… and why.

Eventually, a herniated lumbar disc sealed the deal for me, quelling any lingering hope of a trapeze comeback. I had to crawl down the stairs of my home and was then strapped to a board while an ambulance transported me to my MRI appointment. Thankfully, I recovered but understand that I can't catch anymore.

Dr. Seuss' words come back to me. "Don't cry because it's over, smile because it happened." Life is full of tradeoffs and compromises. As a child, adored by my parents and two siblings, life's glory seemed boundless. The stark reality of adolescence hit, and I began to realize my limitations. I think that contentment comes from doing the best with what we're given. As children, we're often lovingly fed ideas that belie this theory. My family loved watching the movie *Willy Wonka and the Chocolate Factory*. At the end, Willy tells Charlie, "Don't forget what happened to the man who got everything he always wanted. He lived happily ever after." However, the reality is that our time on this planet is full of peaks and valleys. I learned this hard truth, even after overcoming great odds to reach the Ringling dream. I'm glad I established a life outside of the circus. Now I can periodically peer back into this world that I was once a part of and hold a greater appreciation of it.

The circus has been referred to as "show business boot camp," but I never thought of it that way. As I grew older, I came to adopt a greater appreciation for those daring, hardworking, and adventurous men and women who built such a longstanding tradition. For a while, at a very formative time in my life, I was able to stand on their shoulders. The traditional circus fades, but there are shows that manage to continue. I like to think that as I write this, some boy or girl sits and watches, mesmerized as I was.

Maybe he or she will even get to go on the road and become a part of it for a while. Wherever you are, Yakima or Zürich, God bless you. You're in for the adventure of a lifetime. Drink deeply of this splendid journey. It's fleeting.

I can't go back to the reckless abandon I experienced with Carson & Barnes, splendor of being in the Ringling Brothers and Barnum & Bailey Circus, or the muscular precision of catching on the trapeze. There's the proverbial story about the boy who didn't want to leave the circus. Admittedly, part of me wanted to stay in that world forever. I fantasized about being a happy-go-lucky cherub, somehow finding a way to make a living in the world of spangles and sawdust. However, I would have become older. And alas, an aging cherub is a cherub no longer. Nevertheless, since leaving this world full-time at twenty, I've managed some brief circus stints, though not all of them were satisfying. I ceased to be paid for my clowning at Lima's Coliseo Amauta and was bruised and scraped in a performance at a park in Pahrump, Nevada. Such experiences serve as harsh reminders that this world can be a cruel one. I'm glad that my last performance experience was peaceful, tucked into a tent in Lima's San Miguel district. I had time to reflect on the long climb.

I hope a quantity of people will read this work and adopt an appreciation for a culture, the traditional circus, that is slipping away. Life itself is change. Maybe, somebody will be encouraged through this work to pursue his or her dream, whatever it may be. I learned, through the rocky path of a mudshow and Clown College that it's possible for a dream to come true. I also learned that dreams could fall short; I never did catch the triple.

Dreams are limitless and timeless. Alas, muscles, neurons, and tendons aren't. I am aware that the inevitable, gradual diminishing of my physical skills would have eventually forced me out. I wouldn't want to have left that way. Circus performance is a young person's game. Now, when I see a show, I acknowledge resignedly the younger individuals living the dream in tights and rhinestones.

As much as I loved the world of the circus, I am glad that I built a parallel life. The stability I now have through more conventional academic and career pursuits has afforded me the opportunity, I believe, to deepen my affection for the circus world.

The Ringling Brothers and Barnum & Bailey Circus is now over for everybody, not just me. On May 21, 2017, the company graciously streamed the last performance for free. I gazed at my laptop and wept. A kid on the flying trapeze attempted a quadruple somersault. He missed.

While I may step away for years on end, the circus is always entwined in my life. It comforts me to know that it's still out there, somewhere, in some form. For a while I was allowed to make this dream my life. It may never happen again, but the circus always holds a place in my heart. Love can be unrequited. At times it seemed that the circus world, while I always adored it, didn't love me back. Nevertheless, I can reflect on golden moments when I was a part of this splendidly strange way of life. I wouldn't have missed it.